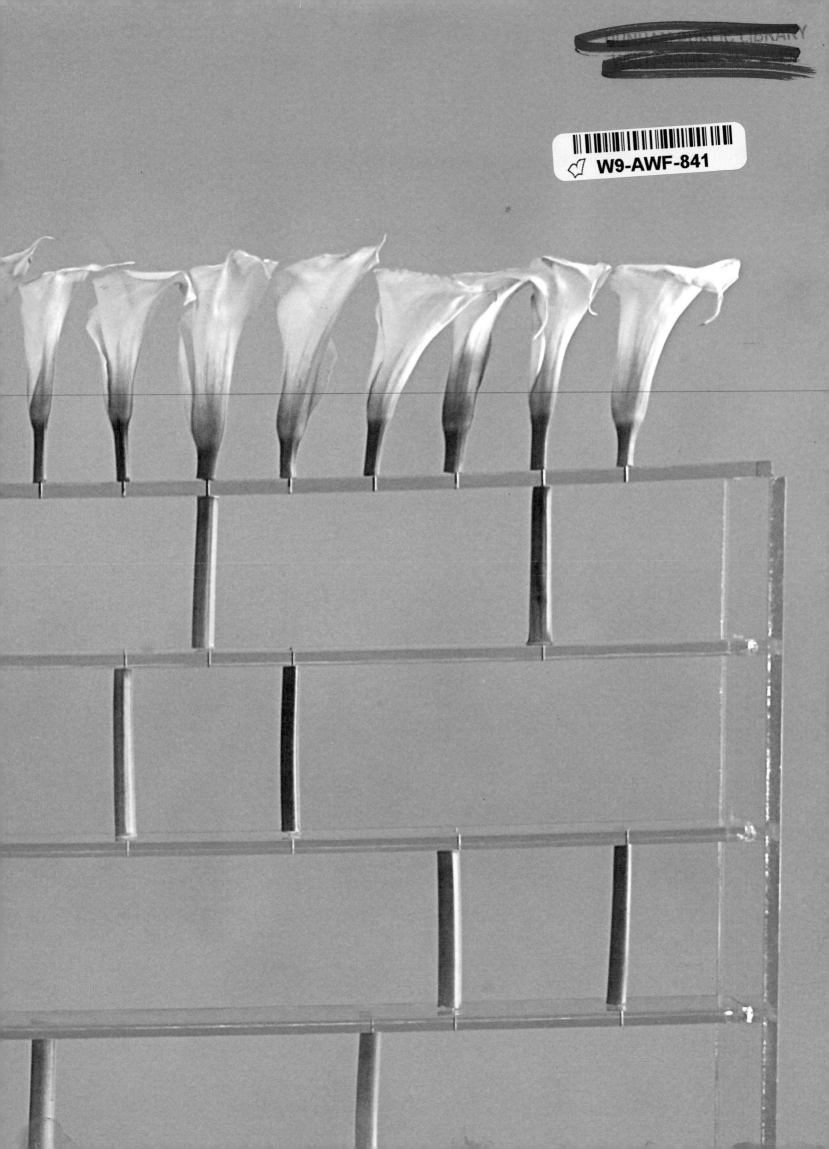

flower arranging

THE AMERICAN WAY

CELEBRATING THE WAFA USA WORLD FLOWER SHOW *THIS GLORIOUS EARTH*

text by NANCY D'OENCH

coordination by DEEN DAY SANDERS

major photography by MICK HALES

flower arranging

THE AMERICAN WAY

A WORLD ASSOCIATION OF FLOWER ARRANGERS (WAFA USA) BOOK

ABRAMS, NEW YORK

contents

It is with great admiration, affection, and gratitude that

WAFA USA

dedicates

FLOWER ARRANGING THE AMERICAN WAY

to

DEEN DAY SANDERS

our muse and friend

introduction

opposite

The medium niche class in the 2008 Philadelphia Flower Show was titled "Crescendo," and two Pennsylvania arrangers, Jane Godshalk of Haverford and Cres Motzi of Downington, said it all with leaves—magnolia leaves. They spent six hours wiring and gluing leaves back-to-back and front-to-front to create the wave. The vase, waiting in Jane's closet for years, carried the brown of the leaves through the design. Yellow light installed in the niche warmed the scene.

*The World Association of Flower Arrangers is a consortium of floral art societies representing thirty countries on six continents. From 2008 through 2011, the United States will be the host country. Among a WAFA host country's duties are covening a teaching seminar and staging a world flower show. WAFA's mission is: education, promotion of floral art, and conservation.

I t has become traditional that the country elected to host the World Association of Flower Arrangers* publish a book celebrating the floral ethos of the land. While *Flower Arranging the American Way* is envisioned as a meaningful souvenir for our international visitors, it also serves a wider purpose as a general introduction to American floral design.

These primarily contemporary works of art have been created by talented amateurs drawn from across the nation. Today, new design ideas travel rapidly from country to country, resulting in a blending of flower arranging styles and techniques. However, there still is a pervading spirit in these designs that is distinctly American.

The arrangers have used plant material native to different climates and terrains in our country, the character of the material reflecting the diversity of our national landscape. Containers may range from rustic pottery to elegant family heirlooms, or may not be used at all. Long-standing conventions governing flower arranging have largely disappeared, yet the basic principles and elements of design are still the backbone of all floral design.

Several design classifications not typically found in flower arranging books have been included. Botanical jewelry and miniatures are American specialties. As the addition of these classes in flower shows has been extremely popular both with the public and arrangers alike, it seemed appropriate to incorporate them here as well. Another new interpretation, Exhibition Tables—tables designed to give just the impression, rather than the reality, of the service of food—also merits a chapter.

While the arrangements are the stars of the book, they would not be able to shine without the illumination of editor Nancy D'Oench's words and the consummate brilliance of Mick Hales's photographic images. We are truly grateful for their patience, perseverance, and sensitivity.

That depictions of arranged flowers have existed since the third millennium B.C. testifies to the tenacity of our art. That our American garden club organizations are both nearing their centennials (The Garden Club of America was founded in 1913 and National Garden Clubs in 1929) is proof of the long-standing love of flowers and flower arranging in this country. It is our privilege to share this sentiment with you through *Flower Arranging the American Way*.

Ruth C. Crocker
President, WAFA

preface

page 2
When wisteria was blooming in her garden, Gail Emmons of Orinda, California, paired it with variegated flax leaves and a peeled and bleached manzanita branch placed horizontally across the top of a tall container. The wisteria blossoms drop naturally, the green of their racemes outlined against the neutral color of the container.

page 4
Five spathes from the queen palm (*Cocos plumosa*) recall the grace of a corps de ballet *en pointe*. Dendrobium orchids, seeded eucalyptus, and a sprinkling of Spanish moss add just the right accompaniment to this design by Janice Hamlin of Bradenton, Florida.

page 5
A double frame of black metal restrains but does not contain an arrangement of orange birds-of-paradise blossoms (*Strelitzia reginae*) and the larger leaves of *Strelitzia nicolai*. Negative space, created by the interplay of frame and plant material, gets equal billing in this design by Ann Tate of Daytona Beach, Florida.

page 6
In this installation by Bliss Clark of Grosse Pointe Farms, Michigan, and Tasha Tobin of Akron, Ohio, palm spathes are joined by a stately member of the lily family, *Eremurus*. The flower, also known as foxtail lily or desert candle, is native to western and central Asia.

From its conception, *Flower Arranging the American Way* had two goals—to commemorate the hosting of the World Flower Show in the United States and to show viewers around the world "the American way" of flower arranging. The latter goal presented some very real challenges—how could we capture representative work of arrangers in the two cooperating organizations and, second, assemble and present the diversity of styles being practiced today?

No one could be better qualified to meet those challenges than Deen Day Sanders, Vice President, Printing and Publications for WAFA USA. Contributing author and organizer of a number of books for National Garden Clubs, Deen began by soliciting names of accomplished arrangers from the Flower Arranging Study Group (FASG) of The Garden Club of America and from the Assembly of Flower Arrangers (AFA) of National Garden Clubs, Inc. In groups of ten or twelve, the arrangers were invited to her home near Atlanta for two-day work sessions, their designs photographed by Mick Hales. In addition, the Creative Floral Arrangers of the Americas (CFAA) held a session in Florida; another group, including members of CFAA and the National Flower Arrangers (NFA) organized a session in Seven Springs, Pennsylvania. Others, either singly or in pairs, had their creations photographed and submitted them; still others sent in photographs taken at earlier flower shows. Mick also photographed designs that interpreted works of art at the Memphis Flower Show. All in all, Deen collected hundreds of images. From that bountiful offering, Margaret L. Kaplan, Editor-at-Large at Harry N. Abrams, Inc., and I selected the 250 presented here. More than one hundred American arrangers—from California to Florida, Michigan to Mississippi—are represented.

The first part of the book, Chapters 1 to 4, focuses on the materials that the designers use, what inspires them—nature's sculptural pieces from the shore and the desert, man-made components complemented by natural materials, and containers that get the creative juices flowing. The arranger's goal, whatever the components, is clarity of design, a simplicity, a rightness. The arranger asks and invites the viewer to question, "Could anything be removed? Does anything need to be added?"

In Chapters 5, 6, and 7, we look at some creative pursuits that are particularly American—complementing works of art with floral designs, exhibition style tables, and the fine art of jewelry making with seeds, beans, and vines. In Chapter 8, the history of flower arranging in America is reviewed, and we see how marvelous masses of flowers—whether in period or startlingly contemporary style—can delight with their abundance. Chapter 9 brings together designs that go "in a new direction," ones that exhibit horizontal and diagonal thrusts. In the final group, Chapter 10, American arrangers work in styles that strike their fancy—parallels, designs in two containers, and the magical world of miniature designs under five inches. Then they explore the ever-expanding world of techniques, even inventing some of their own. Information about how the designs were created and the materials used appears with the photographs. Additional information about styles and techniques is available in books published by the Garden Club of America and the National Garden Clubs, Inc., listed at the back of this volume.

The arrangers in this book certainly are among the most accomplished practitioners of this art in America; each of them, however, would encourage readers to give floral art a try, to discover the increased awareness that comes with tackling this art form, the sensitivity that infuses our lives when eyes are opened to the world around us. An examination of the designs in the early part of the book will reveal that the art is really in seeing the possibilities in the simplest of materials—driftwood, a twist of vine, a curled leaf, even the stalk that once held Brussels sprouts. Once recognized and reclaimed, all that is needed is a way to support or present the piece and then to complement it with fresh or dried plant material.

Nature, in effect, has done much of the creative work for us—in dried material and in a glorious multitude of fresh flowers. Our task is to train our eyes to see, really see, what lies about us. Noticing wood washed ashore on the New England coast inspired Richard Wilbur, former Poet Laureate of the United States, to write "Driftwood," in which he describes pieces as "Warped, wry, but having the beauty of / Excellence earned. . . . [They] have saved in spite of it all their dense / Ingenerate grain." Flower arrangers see that same warped, wry beauty and dense ingenerate grain.

Surely one of the strongest influences on American flower arranging has been ikebana, the Japanese style of flower arranging with its emphasis on the inherent beauty of nature. In Chapter 8, "Marvelous Masses," we see how the open, linear quality of Japanese flower arranging "loosened" the traditional mass, moving it to a line-mass. Other ikebana influences can be found in every chapter, from new techniques to a general sense of daring, a willingness to try something new, totally personal. Gail Emmons, a longtime student of Sogetsu Ikebana, relates the philosophy of the Sogetsu School as taught by Akane Teshigahara, the fourth-generation headmaster of the school, this way: "Sogetsu Ikebana can be created anytime, anywhere, by anyone, in any part of the world, and with any kind of material. Plants are a product of Mother Nature, but Ikebana ultimately reflects the person who arranged it." Surely that thinking has permeated the American way of flower arranging, either consciously or unconsciously.

We invite readers—in any part of the world—to visit and revisit the American way of flower arranging illustrated on these pages, then to try their hands—with any kind of material—at this most rewarding of art forms.

Nancy D'Oench

recognized, reclaimed, recycled

Weathered wood, cactus skeletons, palm spathes, dried vines, gourds, leaves, stalks, pods, lichen, and moss—treasured for their sculptural qualities—are gathered from across our vast land and given new life in the flower arranger's art.

We begin our look at flower arranging in America by focusing on the materials with which arrangers choose to work. Fresh flowers most often take the spotlight and certainly bring a design to life, but the floral artist is by no means limited to the blossoming part of plants. In fact, there is almost no part of a plant, living or dead, that is not raw material for the botanical artist. Weathered wood is an obvious favorite, collected in the hardwood forests that reach across the northern states and the pine barrens of the South. Driftwood is constantly sculpted and polished by the movement of water along the almost 100,000 miles of coastline on the Atlantic and Pacific coasts, the Gulf of Mexico, and the shores of the Great Lakes. In addition, more than 250,000 rivers yield up their treasures for the discriminating and always alert arranger.

The deserts of the southwestern United States are no less generous. Saguaro cacti (*Carnegiea gigantea*) stand like giant, living sculptures in the Sonoran Desert of southern Arizona and extreme southeastern California. Saguaro (pronounced *sah-wah-ro*) often reach twenty to fifty feet tall and live for more than a hundred years. Slow growing, they are uniquely designed to survive the harsh desert climate. Pleated like an accordion, the vertical spines of the saguaro expand in the rainy season and contract in times of drought. Native Americans and early settlers used the spines of dead saguaros in construction; contemporary flower arrangers value the skeletonized arms for their design potential. Dried cholla cacti (*Opuntia*) offer a different and equally intriguing form, their cylindrical length punctured with holes.

Palms, familiar trees in tropical and subtropical climates around the world, present a paint box full of options for the floral artist—fronds, sheaths, spathes, inflorescence, and fruit. The fresh green palm fronds, either palmate (fan-shaped) or pinnate (feather-shaped), lend themselves to clipping and manipulation, and many varieties hold their distinctive forms when dried. Broad sheaths cradle the leaves in some varieties of palms, and as the sheaths age much of the tissue disappears, leaving skeletonized fibers that resemble worn burlap. Spathes that once held the inflorescence and fruit in place take on a woody texture with age and suggest the graceful lines of a long, slim boat. All are salvaged by arrangers and put to artistic use.

In the United States, palms are native to Florida and South Carolina—on whose state flags they appear—and grow successfully as far north as Arkansas, southern Ohio, and Maryland on the East Coast and up to Oregon and Washington, where the temperatures are moderated by the Humboldt Current, on the West Coast.

page 12
Nature was given a hand in "Forward Motion," by Gloria Freitas Steidinger of North Easton, Massachusetts. Two pieces of weathered cedar were glued together, with bits of coconut palm sheaths and dried celosia strategically placed to highlight the sweeping line.

opposite
Wood from a cranberry bog rests on the edge of a pool filled by the waterfall in the background. Designer Sybil Williamson of Greensburg, Pennsylvania, completes the spring scene with blossoms from a Kousa dogwood tree.

Weathered wood, cacti, and palms mark the beginning, but only the beginning, of arrangers' search for interesting forms and textures. No part of a plant—roots, vines, stems, seedpods—dead or alive, eludes the gaze of arrangers. In this section and others you will see bird-of-paradise leaves (*Strelitzia*)—green, smooth, flat, and glossy—presented in their original state but also as dried, rhythmic sculptural forms. Cecropia leaves are a favorite, too, taking on a curled three-dimensional quality when dry and revealing white undersides. Roots and stems of every variety, even stalks that once held dozens of Brussels sprouts, contribute dramatic line and texture to innovative arrangements. Some of the most creative arrangers have recognized the design potential in dead, discarded plant material, reclaimed it from the roadside or compost heap, and recycled it into works of art.

above

The undulating forms of red and green obake anthuriums set this design by Trece Chancellor of Phenix City, Alabama, in motion. A sculpture by Gainesville, Florida, artist Aubrey Griffis supports and circles the blackened wood, creating spaces and repeating the shape of the obakes. A piece of electrical wire painted black and placed in front of the wood continues the rhythm, while aspidistra leaves add depth. *Obake*, a Japanese word for ghost or spirit, refers to the varied shapes and colors these large anthurium hybrids from Hawaii can assume.

below

Bonny Martin of Memphis, Tennessee, lets the wood—sculpted by time and weather, pierced by beetle and bird— be the star in this restrained design. The spaces are left open, their shapes repeated in two calla lilies.

opposite

A powerful piece of weathered wood hovers over a twisted branch, the space between them adding to the tension in the design. Heliconias, anthuriums, and fatsia leaves match the strength of the wood while introducing color and new textures. Diane Herman of Johnstown, Pennsylvania, employs a metal sculpture to support and unite the components.

opposite
Openings in a piece of dried wood found in Florida allow bromeliad blossoms— *Guzmania variegata* 'Pearl' and *Guzmania* 'Vino'—to shine through. Both are cultivar hybrids grown by Lorene Junkin of Gainesville, Florida. Variegated aspidistra and leaves from Pearl brighten the scene.

above
A frame defines the space around a knotted piece of root in this horizontal design by Jeanne Nelson of Congers, New York. Anthurium blossoms and leaves mark the starting point while flax leaves reinforce the visual path, enclosing more space along the way. Jeanne titles this "Stretching One's Imagination."

opposite, left
A cedar root repeats the sharp angles of the container Barbara Willey of Deltona, Florida, has chosen for her design. Sunflowers move from the bottom to the top, with a palm leaf (*Rhapis excelsa*) balancing the space enclosed by the root.

opposite, right
The strength of the mounted wood is carried upward in sunflower stalks, the vertical placement countering the lean of the wood. Sunflower blossoms rotate to the back of this design by Jean Ohlmann of Louisville, Kentucky, and secure the visual balance.

right
Margarette Jones of Houston, Texas, calls this design "High Drama," and for good reason. It stands over eight feet tall (2.36 meters), with palm spathes placed to add height and rhythm to a dramatic piece of driftwood. Obake anthuriums and a leaf of *Monstera deliciosa variegata*, chosen for scale and form, complete the performance.

overleaf, left
In this design by Jean Moran of Farmington, Michigan, a stately piece of wood—polished by the waters of Lake Michigan and bleached on its shores—is complemented by the warm tones of Leonidas roses. The green of viburnum connects the composition to this springtime scene near Atlanta, Georgia.

overleaf, right
The regular branching pattern of a pine tree is still visible in this skeletal form used by designer Pauline Flynn of Port Huron, Michigan, to tell a story. In "Alas! My Broken Heart," Lucite rods curve to create half a heart while a pavéd ball of carnations drops into space. Pauline says crystals and the deep-pink color symbolize hope for renewed love.

opposite

Coral peonies call attention to the ins and outs of weathered wood balanced on a black stand by arranger Joyce Peterson of Pittsburgh, Pennsylvania. Another piece, similar in color but knobby in form, anchors the design on an outcropping of granite.

right

An old tree trunk takes on personality when silhouetted against a dark stone boulder and enhanced with clipped palm fronds. Purple liatris adds another linear form to this design by Diane Hughes of Chalk Hill, Pennsylvania, and the red of gerbera daisies is echoed by the nearby azaleas.

overleaf, left

The lines in a gnarled piece of wood are repeated in the glaze of a ceramic container and in the pleating of cabbage palm fronds, *Sabal palmetto*, Florida's state tree. Inez Brooker of Gainesville, Florida, has introduced white Asiatic lilies for contrast.

overleaf, right

The outer petals of king proteas echo the silver of the branch that weaves through this design by Joyce Droege of Clermont, Florida. Bird-of-paradise leaves (*Strelitzia reginae*) and ginger blossoms (*Alpinia purpurata*) continue the bold forms, while glass tubes with gerberas call attention to the delicate balancing act.

right

With a black vase from Marshall's and a piece of wood collected on a walk with her corgi, Jane Godshalk of Haverford, Pennsylvania, creates "Earth-Inspired Design." Dowels, glued into holes drilled in the wood, reach down into the vase filled with sand. Oasis wedged in and taped to the top holds roses, hydrangea, chinaberry, a bromeliad blossom, and ivy.

opposite

The openings of a monstera leaf are the perfect complement to two skeletonized saguaro arms in a design by Julia Clevett of Powhatan, Virginia. The element of space is further explored in the curled blossoms of calla lilies.

The ribs of a saguaro cactus meet the
pierced skeleton of a dried cholla in
a design titled "Branded" by Brenda
Bingham of Essex Falls, New Jersey.
Twisted barbed wire, an antique
branding iron, and succulents that store
their own water evoke the stark reality of
a cowboy's life in the vast desert of the
American Southwest.

The bleached "fingers" of a saguaro
cactus arm follow the curve of a bold
container in a design by Lois Dupré
Shuster of Champion, Pennsylvania.
The green of *Philodendron selloum*
leaves contrasts with the red blossoms
of heliconia, also known as lobster claw.

The curl of a giant palm spathe is repeated in the clipped form of a cabbage palm frond, two deep-pink ginger blossoms, and a palmate Rhapis leaf. A ceramic container, contemporary in feel, supports this composition by Jean Moran of Farmington, Michigan.

Gloria Freitas Steidinger of North Easton, Massachusetts, features sheaths from the royal palm (*Roystonea* spp.) in her design titled "Royalty." She enhances the natural curl of the sheath by soaking it in water to soften, then wiring it into the desired shape and leaving it to dry. Clipped and curved areca palm fronds add a fresh note of contrast.

opposite

Dried palm fronds, painted the red of fuzzy heliconia blossoms (*Heliconia vellerigera* 'She Kong'), move up the front of the large container, then to the back of the vertical and horizontal stalks, creating multiple planes in this design by Penny Decker of Ormond Beach, Florida. A ball on the left, covered in pussy willow catkins, literally and visually balances the pendant blossom on the right.

right

Here, Royal palm sheaths are combined with the prickly-edged petioles, or leaf stalks, of the Chinese fan palm (*Livistona chinensis*) in an arrangement titled "Sails in the Sunset" by Lorraine Gabler of Grand Island, Florida. A monstera leaf, clipped to create a new form, and pink mink proteas continue the bold lines.

opposite
Two glossy hanging heliconias (*H. rostrata*) in this arrangement by Trece Chancellor of Phenix City, Alabama, are embraced by wisteria vines that match the container in texture and color. A monstera leaf, clipped to accommodate the vine, unites the components. Wisteria is native to the eastern United States and to China, Korea, and Japan.

above
A dried vine on the left and a yucca blossom stalk on the right continue the movement begun in a container from Catalpa Lane Pottery. Mary Poythress of Houston, Texas, has kept the palette soft with proteas of a similar color and just a touch of pink.

below
Jo Ann Wade of Phenix City, Alabama, takes her inspiration from Fred Astaire and Ginger Rogers in this two-part design she calls "Puttin' On the Ritz." Moth orchids (*Phalaenopsis* sp.) and sea grape leaves, painted black and white, represent the elegant dancers while wisteria vine traces their movements.

right

Gourds, bold in form and shiny of surface, are the dominant note in this six-foot-tall design by Lee LaPointe of Vero Beach, Florida. The pierced silhouettes of monstera leaves contrast with the solid forms. Fuzzy heliconias, a variety sometimes called teddy bear heliconia, counter the glossy expanses.

opposite

A painted and carved gourd resembling an exotic bird rests behind clipped papyrus in this design by Carolyn Hawkins of Jonesboro, Georgia. Two other gourds twist and turn on multiple planes around a black tubular armature.

opposite
A seven-foot trunk of saguaro cactus
provides the support, but gourds
steal the show in this composition by
Bobbi Heenan of Jefferson, Georgia.
Heliconias and philodendron leaves
provide contrast in texture and color.
Gourds, while small and still on the vine,
are coaxed into shape and held there
with nylon hose until fully grown. Gourd
shaping is an ancient art, dating from
the Ming dynasty in China, when new
gourds were grown inside clay molds—
some geometrical, some with interior
bas-relief designs. When the gourd was
removed at maturity, it had taken on the
shape and pattern of the mold.

right
Gourds take to water in this
composition with lilies and New Zealand
flax (*Phormium tenax*). Julie Lapham
of Southborough, Massachusetts, has
chosen golden lilies to repeat the warm
tones of the gourds. The lilies' buds lead
the eye from underwater to the upper
reaches of the design.

right

Skeletonized leaves of staghorn fern (*Platycerium* spp.) capture light and complement the color of the container in this design by Melinda Earle of Naples, Florida. Rosettes of flowering kale nestle at the base.

opposite

Dried bird-of-paradise leaves, lower right, continue the embrace begun by loops of skeletonized flax leaves in this arrangement by Carole Bailey of Houston, Texas. The two materials weave in and out of the container, framing a flowerlike succulent and the inflorescence of *Jatropha podagrica*. The latter is also known as the bottleplant or the Buddha belly plant because of its swollen stem.

overleaf, left

Bird-of-paradise leaves (*Strelitzia reginae*) do wonderful things when dried. Here Gloria Freitas Steidinger of North Easton, Massachusetts, has emphasized their sculptural qualities by mounting them on the ends of copper tubing that is curled and screwed to a steel plate. A light spray of copper and green renews their color. A coconut in its husk anchors the design with textural contrast from the inflorescence of a queen palm.

overleaf, right

Helen Goddard of South Dartmouth, Massachusetts, has titled her arrangement "Homage to Paola," a reference to Italian artist Paola Berger, who introduced the sculptural modern mass style to arrangers in the United States in the 1980s. Helen has created a Paola-like design with just two kinds of plant material—dried cecropia leaves (*Cecropia peltata*) and blue hydrangea—the browns in both fusing with the brown of the container.

left
No plant material, however humble, escapes the discerning eye of the flower arranger. Here, lending sculptural form and complex texture to a design by Katrina Vollmer of Nashville, Indiana, are the stalks that are left after Brussels sprouts are removed. Painted black and rising from a glossy black container, they are joined by beehive gingers (*Zingiber spectabilis*) and hosta leaves.

opposite, above
Bonny Martin of Memphis, Tennessee, has left no stone unturned or log unexamined in her search for lichens and mosses of interesting colors and textures. Using a glue gun, she has covered a twenty-four inch Styrofoam ball with an incredible variety. A grapevine cage frames the sphere of many colors, holding it in place.

opposite, below
Leslie Purple of Windmoor, Pennsylvania, has chosen to showcase two tropical seedpods, possibly from the royal poinciana tree (*Delonix regia*). Staged on a polished base and positioned to create space and movement, the pods' curling form is echoed in the fiddlehead ferns and green anthuriums.

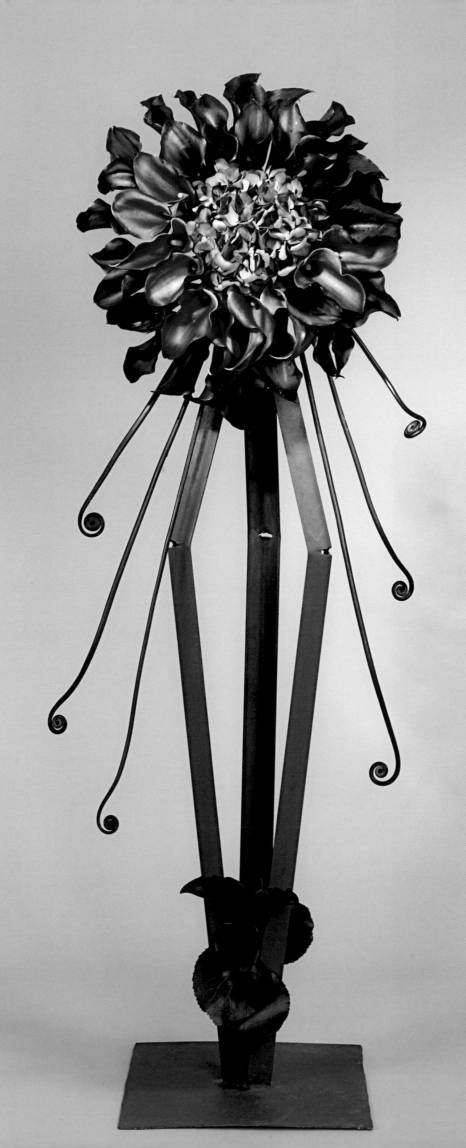

2

forged by man;
complemented by nature

Metals, plastics, and fibers merge with fresh and dried plant material in mixed-media works.

While natural materials are certainly the primary component in the flower arranger's storehouse, they are by no means the only one The artist recognizes the possibilities of form and texture, color and line in metal and plastic, in place mats for the table and racks for CDs. The thrill of the creative process is in spotting an unlikely item—in an unlikely place—that could become part of an innovative design.

Catalogues that come in the mail get more attention than they would otherwise because a treasure might be lurking somewhere in those pages. The aisles of department and discount stores are perused; art galleries are visited; antique shops are scoured—always with an eye to some future, as yet undetermined, arrangement. An old green-glass Chianti bottle, four feet tall and in the shape of a boa constrictor, might be bought on a whim, then left to collect dust in the corner of the garage for twenty years. But when a flower show schedule arrives with a circus theme, and there's a class titled "Side Show," that bottle has just the bizarre quality that's required.

At town dumps, now known as "community recycling centers," the "iron and light-metal" receptacles merit a careful look to see what treasures have been discarded, renewing the adage that one man's trash is another man's treasure. The stand of a floor lamp might support a cascading arrangement; the circular cover of an electric fan might set a design in motion. Case in point: The pieces of Lucite in Penny Horne's design on page 51 were about to land in the trash.

Artists who work in metal, plastic, and other media recognize the market in the flower arranging world and have responded with pieces that offer interesting shapes, many crafted with supports for fresh plant material. Ken Schwartz of West Allis, Wisconsin, and Joy Parker of Bremerton, Washington, are artists whose works appear in this and other sections. Major flower and garden shows and regional garden club events attract vendors with sculptural pieces.

Arrangers often commission structures, working with an artist or a metal shop to get the form and size they envision. Deen Day Sanders had the two triangles featured on page 64 made to order. Margot Paddock, quoted in *The Fine Art of Flower Arranging*, pages 182–83, instructs arrangers on "how to talk to your welder." Margot herself has taken years of welding classes, often building the armatures that support her exceptional designs.

Whatever the material "forged by man," it is the natural plant material that takes center stage, that is the featured player. If fresh flowers are not used, then the form

page 48
Pavé of the highest order characterizes this design by Bonnie Mirmak of Vienna, Virginia, atop an angular armature. Dozens of calla lilies—in coral, burgundy, and black—surround hydrangea blossoms in a symmetrical triumph. Fiddlehead ferns in deepest burgundy reach down, repeating the lines of the metal structure. Galax leaves at the base echo the dark colors of the callas.

opposite
Penny Horne of East Rochester, New York, reclaimed leftover pieces of Lucite from a Rochester theater production. She then recycled them into a precise design that asks the eye to follow each piece of calla stem to its flower at the top. The plant material seems to float in space, but the weightlessness is an illusion. The support is almost four feet long, each shelf one-half-inch thick and four inches wide. Penny describes it as "Furiously heavy!"

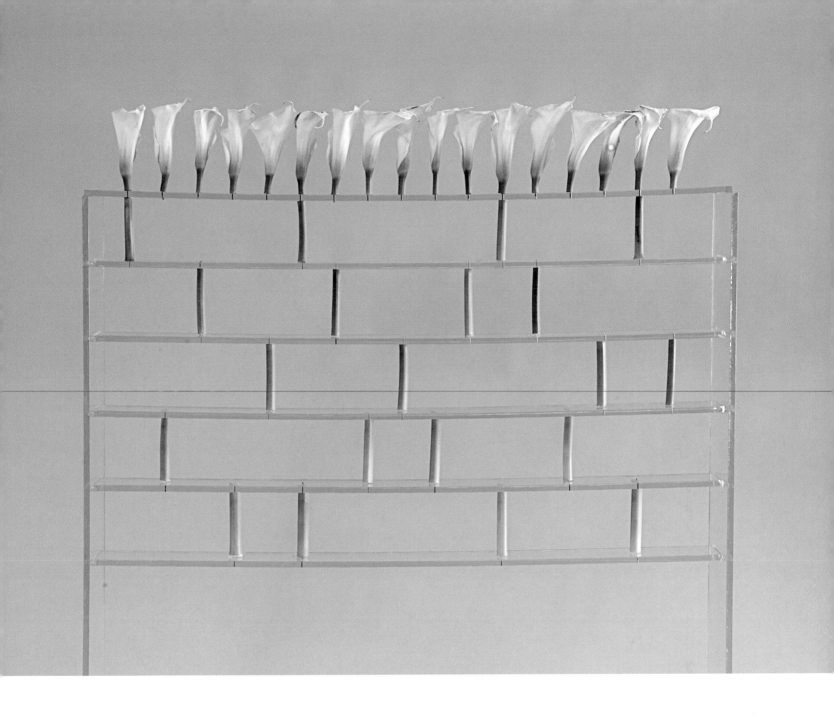

and texture of the dried but natural material take precedence, the man-made material playing a supporting role. Natural forms are so innately compelling that this is not a challenge. Even in Pauline Flynn's design on page 67, the ten-foot-tall angular metal and glass sculpture is balanced and complemented by the enormous yet airy shape of the *Allium schubertii* and the delicate hydrangea petals in the glass tube.

Complement—to complete or make perfect—is the guiding principle in using man-made material. Bonnie Mirmark, page 48, chooses fiddlehead ferns with long dark stems to follow the lines of the black metal stand that supports her pavé of almost black calla lilies. Ann Tate, page 5, uses the angular form of birds-of-paradise to repeat the angles of the frame backing her arrangement.

In the following designs, arrangers use materials forged by man to set the stage for Mother Nature. The form, pattern, texture, and colors of man-made and natural merge in these innovative designs.

opposite

A Lucite sculpture by Joy Parker sits atop a Lucite box holding the first of a parade of green anthuriums kissed with warmer coral tones. Helen S. Martin of Florence, South Carolina, has repeated the colors but varied the forms on the opposite side of the sculpture with green and pink amaranthus. She titles the design "Love Lies Bleeding," another name for the amaranthus.

right

Holes are made to be filled—or left empty. Helen Goddard of South Dartmouth, Massachusetts, does a bit of each in this motion- and tension-filled design. A brittle, crumpled cecropia leaf blows one way; soft, pristine lilies rotate in the opposite direction. The strength of the black metal form unifies the components.

overleaf, left

Julia Clevett of Powhatan, Virginia, has used a variety of man-made materials in her composition that emphasizes angles—in the frames, pieces of Lucite, and even in the supporting form. But there are circles, too, in that support and in the swirling lines within the frames. Variegated ti leaves (*Cordyline fructicosa* 'Kiwi') unite the elements and reflect the colors of the Lucite.

overleaf, right

This basket was designed to hold a candle in its base. Tasha Tobin of Akron, Ohio, has used its wires to "entrap" green cymbidium orchids, Banksias (Australian members of the Protea family), lily grass, and dried reeds. The stems emerge from both sides of the cagelike structure in a design Tasha calls "Gridlock."

left

Marsha Webb of Sandy Springs, Georgia, says she found the pagodalike form in a consignment shop and believes it was originally a lawn sculpture. She is also recycling a child's toy, a red plastic foam tube with a wire inside, to which she has attached dried palm fronds. The small red form is dried, painted plant material that was bought under the name "spider cone" but has so far defied further identification. The whole comes together with the graceful rhythm of a Balinese dancer.

opposite

In an arrangement inspired by artist Isamu Noguchi (1904–1988), who also designed furniture and lighting, an inverted umbrella stand holds a ceramic container while another, with Noguchi-like flowing lines, sits at the bottom. The undulating forms of anthurium blossoms and leaves complete this composition by Peggy Nuse of Ormond Beach, Florida.

overleaf, left

Arrangers love metal sculptures by Ken Schwartz of West Allis, Wisconsin. Liz Murken of Oshkosh, Wisconsin, has taken one of his creations and raised it to another level with the simple addition of two dried allium heads, *Allium schubertii*, painted red with black stems to match the sculpture. No small design, this—*A. schubertii* blossoms can measure eighteen inches across.

overleaf, right

Ena McGrattan is an Irish arranger who has embraced her new home in Fort Myers, Florida, with enthusiasm. This design is titled "Florida Orange Slice" and features a metal stand with semicircular shapes. Ena has filled the "slices" with orange sisal, a fiber from the agave plant, long used for carpeting, roping, and insulation, that is now available in colored sheets—for flower arrangers. Red-and-yellow heliconias, placed in front of and behind the stand, add depth, as does the grouping of fig leaves.

opposite

The pink and black of pink mink proteas reminded Jan Sillik of Jacksonville, Florida, of "Prom Night." Dance steps begun in the rotation of the three-part container continue in loops of black cable (actually ski-tow rope), aspidistra leaves, and lily grass. The number of dancers seems to dwindle as the evening comes to an end.

right

Nancy Passfield of Port Sanilac, Michigan, has threaded a flexible black metal sculpture onto a Lucite rod, creating a design that is rhythmic from every angle. Boston ferns and bicolored roses, named "Exciting," establish a focal point but let the eye follow the sculpture's curves.

overleaf, left

An elliptical explosion of metal rods backs a rustic piece of wood and the multiple bracts of a red, yellow, and green heliconia blossom in this composition by Penny Decker of Ormond Beach, Florida. A philodendron leaf adds its own pierced silhouette to the openings in the metal structure and the wood, and a second heliconia drops over the back, creating yet another plane of interest.

overleaf, right

Three highly reflective silver wall plaques are mounted on a metal sculpture in this composition by Lillian Rico of Guaynabo, Puerto Rico. The bold, glossy forms of heliconia blossoms and leaves hold their own against the angles and textures of the man-made material.

opposite

Deen Day Sanders commissioned these bold aluminum frames with holes to accommodate plant material. Here, a honeysuckle vine ties together groupings from her garden—pink hydrangea blossoms and hellebore leaves backed by philodendron—in a design of intriguing spaces and fluid motion on multiple levels. Deen has named the installation "Trinity," and it seems very much at home in her Duluth, Georgia, garden.

above

The Pennsylvania sky lights up this design by Marilyn Whitmore of Bedford, Pennsylvania. A sharply angled sculpture begins a rotation continued by allium blossoms and hosta leaves. Branches of fantail willow repeat the color of the metal and add a new texture.

below

Designer Barbara Eckstein of Pittsburgh, Pennsylvania, invites you to "Look Closely" at this composition, which uses a metal structure of circles to support various materials, including red anthuriums, sweetgum branches (*Liquidambar*), and yellow billy balls (*Craspedia*). The transparency of a sea fan at the top allows the silver of a granite boulder to shine through.

65

above left

Where does an aluminum sculpture by Ken Schwartz stop and the roped lighting added by arranger Diane Herman of Johnstown, Pennsylvania, begin? The mystery is a compliment to both artists. Hosta leaves anchor the base, and the dense blossoms of *Allium christophii* repeat the round spaces created by the loops of aluminum and lighted roping.

above right

A metal armature supports bleached wood and the massive blossoms of white birds-of-paradise (*Strelitzia nicolai*) in this design by Carol Lucia of Seminole, Florida. Sea-blue netting emerges from the stalk of a palm inflorescence, repeating the lines and color of the sculpture, adding depth to the composition.

opposite

Lengths of square metal tubing have been welded at varying angles into a sculptural piece that dares an arranger to use it. Pauline Flynn of Port Huron, Michigan, received this challenge from a flower arranging friend and had her son add a few more twists and turns. She then inserted two glass tubes, acquired at a recycling yard. One she has patiently filled with fresh florets from a hydrangea; the other contains 7-Up, chosen by Pauline for its slight effervescence and assured clarity. A giant *Allium schubertii* blossom, grown, dried, and painted by the arranger, packs enough punch to balance the man-made components.

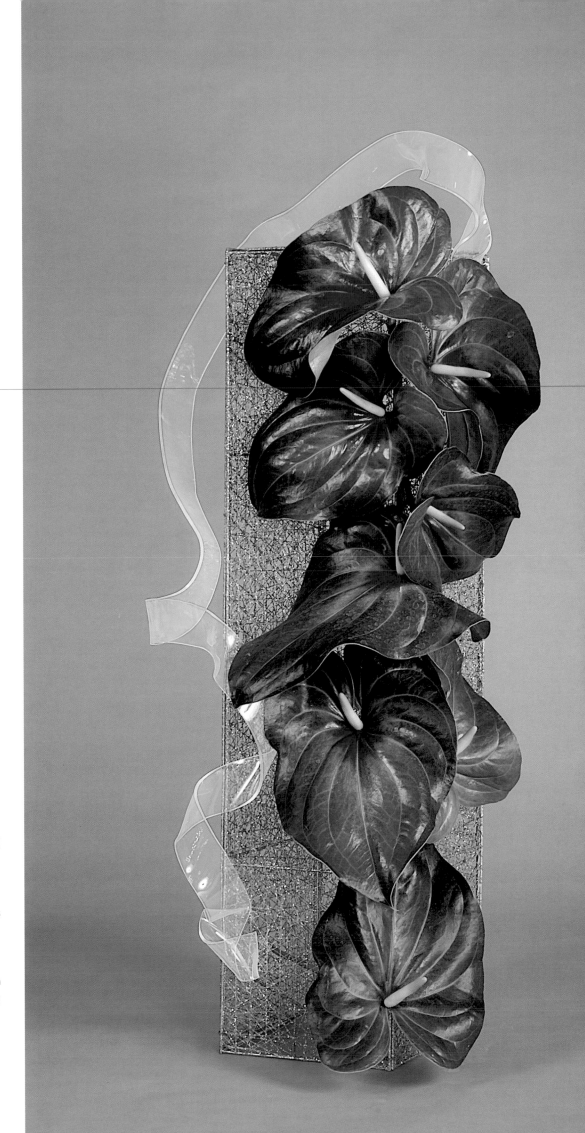

opposite

Black and gray squares and circles are pierced by a bright pink Lucite rod and Plexiglas ribbon in this design by Betty Grimes of Hiawassee, Georgia. Silvered palm and dried, painted protea punctuate the composition. As a name for this design, Betty suggested, "Once I was square; now I'm jumpin' with jazz."

right

A lime-green ribbon of plastic heightens the undulation of the deep-green-and-red anthuriums that dance along a gold mesh form. Marsha Webb of Sandy Springs, Georgia, has varied the position of each blossom, dramatically increasing the sense of movement in the design.

left

The shiny metal sculpture is similar in size and gloss to the bird-of-paradise leaves (*Strelitzia reginae*) that loop through it. Orange "birds" that fan out of the strelitzia bracts are almost the same size as the openings in the sculpture. Cindy Rieger of Fort Lauderdale, Florida, plays plant material against man-made in this melding of color, texture, and pattern.

opposite

No component—man-made or natural—escapes the discerning eye of the experienced arranger. Here, plant material has been shaped by man into place mats—and chosen by arranger Tony Todesco of Stow, Massachusetts, for a study he titles "Green on Green." Rosettes of echeveria, ascending toward a cluster of smaller succulents, repeat with subtle variation the color, form, and complex texture of the mats. Pandanus leaves, bent at a sharp angle, present a bolder contrast, while a metal armature supports the whole.

inspiration? it's in the container

Fine glass and pottery pieces get equal billing
in designs that unite plant material and
container in an artistic whole.

A number of years ago, a relatively new arranger was struggling with a
design for a flower show. She asked a friend and mentor for advice.
The more experienced arranger took one look at the effort and said,
"What you need is a good container."

There was a wealth of wisdom in those few words. A good container is a good
beginning—possibly the very best beginning—for contemporary flower arrangements.
In traditional arrangements, the container may suggest a particular period or a color
that will predominate in the final arrangement, but ultimately the vase or urn takes a
back seat to the mass of plant material. In a contemporary arrangement, the container
can be quite prominent, sometimes even dominant. It can be a work of art in its own
right—from glass artist or ceramist—and may need only to be complemented with
plant material in the color, texture, or form already present in the container's design.
In other words, finding the right container may mean that the arrangement is well on
its way to completion.

In the designs that follow, you will see examples in which the container begins a
line that is so effectively continued with a vine or other plant material that the viewer
must look twice to see where the container stops and the vine starts. Liz Murken's and
Jo Ann Wade's designs on pages 79 and 80 illustrate this point.

While the container contributes greatly to the success of a design, it also makes
its demands. The shape and size, the texture, the very feel of the container must be
respected in choosing the other components. The visually heavy brown vase in Gail
Emmons's design on page 75 is balanced by the weighty brown palm inflorescence
in the top of the design. Sometimes the form of a particular plant material echoes
the form of the container so perfectly that it would seem they were made for each
other, as is the case in Gay Estes's combination on page 77, with rattler ginger echoing
the rotating pleats of the container. A particular color or form in the container sends
the arranger in search of plant material that will repeat that quality. If the color does
not exist, then a can of paint may come to the rescue, as it does so effectively in Gail
Emmons's design (page 72) with the red branches. If the container's form is elusive
in natural plant material, then manipulation—bending, looping—may be in order, as
illustrated in Cecilia Lindemann's design on page 93.

The value of a good container is well illustrated here, but where do arrangers
find pieces like the ones featured on these pages? There's probably a story behind
the acquisition of each and every container, but if a survey were taken, a number of

page 72

"The container is the reason for this
design," according to Gail Emmons
of Orinda, California, and once Gail
complemented it with red mitsumata
branches and green anthurium, it's hard
to imagine it holding anything else. The
almost equal attraction of the anthurium
and the glass container creates tension,
while the backward thrust of the
branches explores depth.

opposite

Gail Emmons explains her choices
in this Sogetsu freestyle this way:
"The container and the dried palm
inflorescence were my inspiration.
They had the same rough feeling and
movement, and I felt putting the orchids
and aspidistra with them was a nice
contrast in texture and color."

sources would appear repeatedly. Certainly, some of the pieces are from galleries that feature handcrafted pottery or from vendors at flower shows and regional meetings who specialize in the shapes and surfaces that arrangers covet. David and Keiko Hergesheimer of Catalpa Lane Pottery in Yellow Springs, Ohio, have a devoted following. Perhaps more surprising but frequently mentioned sources are Marshall's, Home Goods, T. J. Maxx, Target, and similar stores, followed closely by thrift shops, antique/junque shops, and tag sales. In other words, any place is a good place to find a great container. In the flower arranger's mind, all of the above sources merit frequent checking; you never know what you might find.

A good container holds more than water and plant material; it holds that most treasured of flower arranging components—inspiration!

opposite

Twisted monkey puzzle vine connects two containers and repeats the lines that zigzag around them. Red heliconias edged in yellow recall the container's touches of red and yellow in this design by Elizabeth Shaw of Gainesville, Florida.

above

The ascending lines on this container reminded Gay Estes of Houston, Texas, of the impossible staircases drawn by graphic artist M. C. Escher. She compounded the illusion with descending yellow rattlers (*Calathea crotalifera*). Looped leaves of another variety of calathea offer a place to pause on the stairways.

above

Before a single flower is placed in it, this ceramic container is a symphony of line, movement, and space. Bonny Martin of Memphis, Tennessee, heard the music and added the voices of pincushion protea, miniature calla lilies, and lily grass. The resulting rhythm and enclosed spaces mesmerize the eye and engage the mind.

opposite

Where does the container stop and the plant material begin? Wisteria vine from Jo Ann Wade's Phenix, Alabama, garden emerges from and follows the lines of the handmade container, then moves out and up, enclosing space and adding its own contortions. Pink ginger blossoms and foliage join the dance.

overleaf, left

A neighbor gave Liz Murken of Oshkosh, Wisconsin, the branch after it fell on her lawn. Liz bought the container at the United States National Arboretum in Washington, D. C., while attending a garden club meeting. A thousand miles apart, yet clearly meant for each other, branch and container merge into one. Two foxtail lilies, philodendron, and variegated dracaena leaves balance the upward thrust of the strong line.

overleaf, right

Lengths of horsetail (*Equisetum*) follow the angles of the container in this design by Gilda de Garcia of McAllen, Texas, and Tampico, Mexico. The stalks and blossoms of heliconia contribute their own angles and a contrast in color and texture.

left
A brushlike pattern on a handmade container suggested the movement and color of palm boots (leaf bases) to Liz Murken of Oshkosh, Wisconsin. Mullein stalks continue the color and alter the texture, while princess proteas (*Protea grandiceps*) balance the bold forms.

opposite
A container—with circles and vertical and diagonal lines—presents the challenge. Harriet Osborne of Baton Rouge, Louisiana, responds with the diagonal thrust of New Zealand flax, the vertical lines of Asiatic lilies, and the convolutions of kiwi vine, suggesting but not replicating the circles.

above

A yellow ikebana container suggested the tropical material in this Ohara School free-style design by Jeannette Arrington of Greenville, South Carolina. Croton leaves, dracaena, and a bromeliad blossom follow the rocking lines and repeat or complement the sunny color.

opposite

The triangle in the wood mirrors the triangle in the container in an arrangement by Claudia Chopp of Wentzville, Missouri. Striations in the wood and container are reflected in the variegation of the ti leaves, which also echo the color of the roses.

opposite
The rounded form of the container called
for rosettes of flowering kale, while the
mottled leaves of sansevieria seemed
a perfect match to its speckled surface.
Karen Hall of DeLand, Florida, added a
twist of weathered wood for contrast and
continued rhythm.

above
Pink slipper orchids (*Paphiopedilum*
'*Magic Lantern*') appear ready to move
into the just-the-right-size opening of this
circular ceramic container and emerge
again amidst the maidenhair fern. Bonny
Martin of Memphis, Tennessee, has used
a minimum of components in an elegant,
serene design.

above

The texture of the container is intensified in prickly pods, while the callas and dried leaves follow the rounded line. Carol Swift of Lake Forest, Illinois, has maintained a subtle autumn palette in responding to the ceramic container.

opposite

Gay Estes of Houston, Texas, has never met a challenge she did not relish. When faced with a rough piece of pottery pierced through with nails, she visited an Asian market and came back with ginger, mushrooms, and other exotica, all in the brown-to-white tones of the container. A dried banana blossom tops the design and a vine weaves in and out of the openings. Nails in the ginger remind the viewer of the original inspiration.

opposite
Tony Todesco of Stow, Massachusetts, sees opportunity where some may see a void, filling one glass column with five golden apples, one with two pears and an apple, and leaving the third with crystal clear water. Clipped sago palm, monstera leaves, and lucky bamboo (*Dracaena sanderiana*) continue the ascent begun by the fruit.

left and above
In a design that Bliss Clark of Grosse Pointe Farms, Michigan, titles "Reflections," the top group of irises appears to be mirrored on the surface of the container. The lower irises are in fact suspended upside down in the water, with hydrangea blossoms concealing the supporting Oasis and continuing the blue. A slight turn (above), and the container, with its rounded corners, compounds the illusion. Now the lower group appears to be two or more. Who said there's no magic in clear glass!

left
A tall, glossy black container needed a gourd of like color, texture, and volume to continue its line. Leslie Purple of Wyndmoor, Pennysylvania, put together this winning combination, then added a vine, bells of Ireland, and anthuriums to keep the rhythm going.

opposite
A triangle here, a triangle there. Two loops, with space between them, here; two more there. The inspiration for this design by Cecile Lindemann of St. Charles, Missouri, is abundantly clear and satisfying. Steel grass and flax provide the geometric forms while three placements of white hydrangea touched with blue add depth to the arrangement.

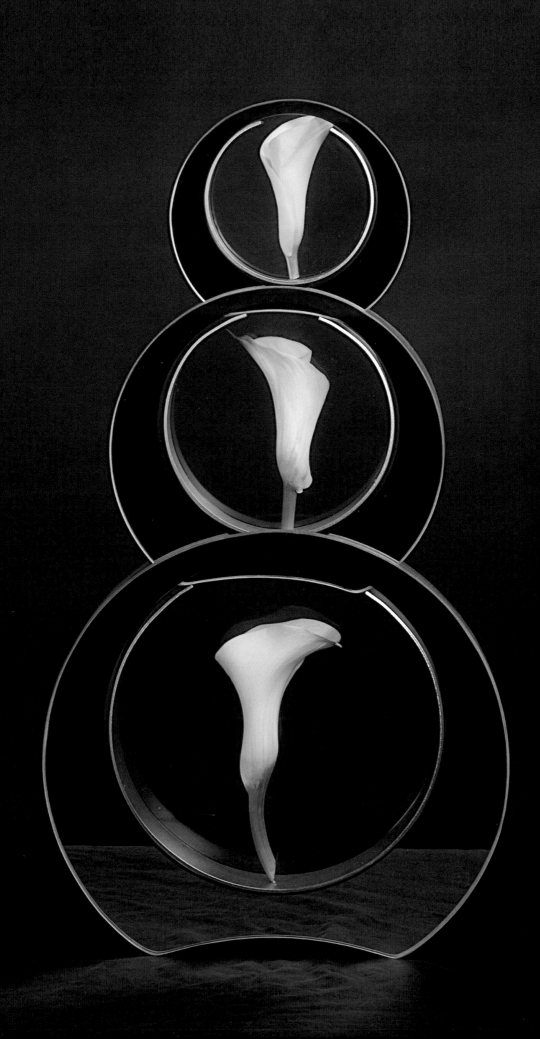

one component, many ideas

Arrangers, working at different times with the same components, show that creativity can move in many directions.

pages 94, 97
Hard to believe, but the containers in these two pictures are the same. The angle, the light, the background make all the difference and testify to the art and magic of photographer Mick Hales. Margot Paddock of Pittsfield, Massachusetts, stacked the three containers (page 94) and added to the mystery by suspending a calla lily in each one. But how? What holds the lilies erect? Margot explained that the round centers, which appear to be empty spaces, are actually glass containers. The callas are carefully braced against the sides. A frontal shot against a black background makes the whole transparent rather than reflective. Shot from a high angle (page 97), the surface of the containers reflects light, creating a mirror effect in the design by Katrina Vollmer of Nashville, Indiana. Pink peonies and ti leaves inserted at a bold angle complete the contemporary picture.

I n the last chapter we saw creative arrangements inspired, in large part, by the intrinsic design qualities of the containers—line, color, surface texture, visual weight. On the following pages we see how one container or component can inspire multiple creative designs.

Many of the photographs in this book were made during flower arranging sessions at Deen Day Sanders' home near Atlanta, Georgia. About a dozen experienced arrangers at a time were invited to attend two-day workshops. They were encouraged to bring plant material and components in order to create favorite designs. When those arrangements were finished and photographed, arrangers were free to make other designs, using containers and other components from Deen's collection.

To say that Deen has a wonderful collection—of containers, dried material, and varied components—does not begin to paint the picture. One arranger said she felt she had landed in Aladdin's cave; others described the experience as one of having died and gone to flower arrangers' heaven. It was almost impossible to choose, to know where to begin. But begin they did. This chapter, for the most part, shows how arrangers in different sessions chose a particular component—and went in entirely different directions. One small pottery piece with multiple openings spoke to four arrangers (see pages 108–9).

Arabella Dane, Claudia Chopp, and Katrina Vollmer each picked up the elk horns (pages 126–27) in Deen's collection. Claudia formed them into a "vase" that cradled sunflowers and woodsy material. Arabella stacked the horns, interweaving a green and orange line—apples, oranges, leucodendron, monstera, and fatsia leaves. Katrina used the points of the antlers to support a dramatic horizontal design of red ginger and peach-colored peonies. Attending different sessions at Deen's, these designers won't know what the others did until they see this book.

Two bits of wood met with equally enthusiastic approval. One was a knotty, curled piece shown on pages 118–19; the other was a sharply angled "elbow," pages 120–21. The treatments of the wood are so different that the viewer has to look closely to determine that they are indeed the same pieces, turned up and down, left and right. The curled piece is complemented, in three different designs, with three very different flowers—coral peonies in one, white lilies in a second, and sunflowers stripped of their petals in a third. The "elbow" received equally varied treatment, more evidence of the limitless creativity of flower arrangers.

Even though being at Deen's and having access to the treasures she has collected over a span of thirty-five years was a unique experience, there is often a particular class in flower shows that showcases this kind of creativity—what different arrangers can come up with, given the same materials with which to work. Called a challenge class, it may be an invitational class for judges who have traveled a great distance and will be judging other arrangements in the show. Each entrant is given exactly the same components—container, mechanics, plant material, and anything else that the committee thinks will make for an interesting challenge—from Slinkys to seed packets, depending on the title of the class. In a limited amount of time, usually two hours, exhibitors create original compositions that are then judged—by other judges—according to the elements and principles of design.

Some flower arrangers' workshops operate on a similar principle, with ten, twenty, thirty, or more participants using the same components and following their own creative instincts. The no-two-alike results are stimulating and singularly instructive. We think you will find the same true of the designs that follow.

left

One container, a fairly simple one of muted colors with horizontal indentations, has taken three accomplished arrangers in entirely different directions. A line-mass design of all green material was the response of Mary Webster of Palm Beach, Florida. Fern, equisetum, bells of Ireland, peppers, and even a couple of green apples are placed at an angle to take advantage of the container's height.

opposite, above

Gay Estes of Houston, Texas, saw architectural potential in the container and created a minimalist salute to Chicago, the city of broad shoulders. The mitsumata branches are split to create the appearance of piercing the container. Calla lilies soar above "clouds" of white fiber.

opposite, below

Carole Bailey of Houston, Texas, took her cue from the indentations and created a contemporary horizontal design underpinned with weathered wood similar in color to the container. Green cymbidium orchids, white hydrangea, and anthurium blossoms are sheltered by the skeletonized leaves of a rubber plant.

overleaf, left and right

Susan Detjens of Sheffield, Massachusetts, and Mary Webster of Palm Beach, Florida, were both enchanted by the ropelike line that wraps around this double container. Susan followed it with hosta leaves, repeating its curve with loops of bear grass and brightening the scene with coral peonies. Mary accented the roping with the almost black leaves of an alocasia. The burgundy of the leaves' underside is repeated in the calla lilies and fiddlehead ferns.

opposite
Linda Nelson of Keiser, Oregon, and Lynn
Laufenberg of Waukesha, Wisconsin, were
both attracted to a round black container.
Linda followed its line with black alocasia
leaves and a wrinkled, dried gourd. Space
in palm spathes repeated the open space
in the container's base.

above
In Lynn's design an alocasia leaf follows
the container's curve and leads to a piece
of weathered root that looks as though it
could walk and pull the container with it.
Nandina berries and anthurium blossoms
counter the pull.

left

A cluster of pink mink protea and
dark foliage—alocasia, phormium,
cordyline—teeters on one side of a
square container in a design by Margot
Paddock of Pittsfield, Massachusetts.
A single phormium leaf drops down,
sustaining balance and echoing the
space in the center of the container.

opposite

Jo Ann Wade of Phenix City, Alabama,
combines two of the containers, altering
the scale and creating new spaces.
Weathered, fasciated wood emphasizes
the rough texture of the two squares,
while touches of green hydrangea
foliage provide contrast. Pink-and-white
hydrangea blossoms appear to be lit
from within.

A container similar to the previous one
but with added angles and openings
"spoke" to three different arrangers.
A horizontal arrangement by Susan
Detjens of Sheffield, Massachusetts,
reaches out from the container with
linear leaves—sansevieria, phormium,
and variegated aspidistra. Glossy
magnolia leaves frame a cascade of pink
ginger and small heliconia.

opposite, below
A piece of weathered wood follows the
lines of the container in a contemporary
design by Linda Nelson of Keizer,
Oregon. Small, golden beehive gingers
march up the left side of the container;
two larger gingers on the right create
interest and tension. Clipped monstera
leaves follow the rhythm established by
the wood.

right
Margot Paddock of Pittsfield,
Massachusetts, filled one opening with
birds-of-paradise, papyrus, alocasia, and
galax leaves, carrying a bit of the plant
material to a second opening.

opposite

One container, four creative minds. The slight variations in color in the angular container inspired Marsha Webb of Sandy Springs, Georgia, to explore the variegations in plant material—flowering kale, sansevieria, aspidistra, hosta, phormium, and reeds.

above

Trece Chancellor of Phenix City, Alabama, used the multiple openings to create a rotating effect with weathered wood and a piece of palm sheath. Flowering kale and green callas continue the rhythm.

center

Kitty Larkin of Menomonee Falls, Wisconsin, looked at the container and saw horizontal possibilities in a design titled "Reaching Out." Purple liatris pierce the openings and appear again above the container, supported by white mitsumato branches. Roses and arching eucalyptus connect the two layers.

below

A commanding piece of weathered wood emerges from one of the openings in a design by Shirley Nicolai of Fort Washington, Maryland. *Nandina domestica* berries tumble down the front and a cluster of variegated osmanthus foliage arises from the back. The three textures create interest while the massing complements the visual weight of the container.

left
Gay Estes of Houston, Texas,
may have been making a fashion
statement. She says she saw the
sinuous shape, the pure line, and
implied motion as sophisticated
glamour with an Asian touch, à la
Vera Wang. A banana blossom
carries the tight line and color,
while beaded fibers add the bling.

opposite
Continuing the motion begun in
the gourd container, Lucinda Seale
of Jasper, Texas, sends loops of
bear grass into space and back
again, sheltering anthuriums the
color of the container. Anthurium
and fatsia leaves counter the bend
of the container.

opposite, above
The texture and color of a simple brown
container set in motion the creative minds
of three arrangers. For Melinda Earle of
Naples, Florida, a particular kind of cecropia
leaf *(Cecropia palmata)* that dries brown
on both sides seemed the perfect match.
White lilies with just a touch of brown in
the stamens were added for direction
and contrast.

opposite, below
The sequinlike band that echoes the
ribbing in the container is actually
composed of dozens of glycerinized leaves
in this arrangement. Mary Jo Strawbridge
of Merion Station, Pennsylvania, taped
two heavy wires to the back of a strip of
birch bark, applied double-sided tape
to the front, and then added the leaves
one by one. Swirling branches and obake
anthurium stand out against the dark
outline of a fatsia leaf and the black
background.

above
"Well met" certainly describes this
arrangement by Gretchen Riley of
Haverford, Pennsylvania, and this setting.
The warm colors of the brick wall are
repeated in the container and the wood,
walnuts, palm spathes, and seedpods of
the design. Green and white anthurium
and fern fronds reflect the many greens of
the spring scene around this Georgia lake.

opposite
Faced with the same abstract animal form, two arrangers chose to "dress" it differently. Mary Ellen O'Brien of Sheffield, Massachusetts, chose the green/black alocasia known as African mask to accent the shape of the container. The shape of the heliconia bracts echoes the markings in the leaves, and the green/black tips carry the dark color through the design.

above
Arabella Dane of Center Harbor, New Hampshire, paints a picture in vibrant reds, yellows, and greens with parrot tulips, ti leaves, and celosias. Fiddlehead ferns repeat the curves of the ceramic form.

overleaf, left above
Two arrangers found green an obvious choice for a container with a band of green glaze. Charlyne Harrison of Atlanta, Georgia, chose green anthuriums and continued the color and motion of the container with a palm infloresence and spathe.

overleaf, left below
Mary Jo Strawbridge of Merion Station, Pennsylvania, compounded the green and the motion with bells of Ireland, swirls of green twig dogwood, green and pink anthurium, and hydrangea with a touch of green.

overleaf, right, above and below
One component, in this case an arc of polished wood, can send a single arranger exploring design possibilities. In the first design, Helen Martin of Florence, South Carolina, extends the line of the wood with green anthuriums that also reflect the gloss of the piece. In the second arrangement, the wood is in the same position but backed by a triangle of carnations in light and dark pink. Modified triangles, green anthuriums touched with pink, are placed to the front.

opposite, above and below

A gnarled piece of wood caught the attention of at least three arrangers. Jackie Payne of Alpharetta, Georgia, and Mary Webster of Palm Beach, Florida, each paired it with a black container, letting the end extend out and down. Jackie introduced a cecropia leaf that repeats the curl in the wood and white lilies with green centers. Clipped palm fronds follow the line of the wood. Mary Webster emphasized the warm tones with coral peonies, looped leaves of aspidistra, and a bit of ruscus.

above

Carole Bailey of Houston, Texas, chose a different container and a very different look. Placing the wood on the outside, she chose an even stronger form—a dried yucca stalk—as the dominant component. Sunflower heads, stripped of all petals save one, and a dried strelitzia leaf curled around the rim complete the somber picture. What would you name this arrangement? Carole has suggested "Day's Last Breath" or "Global Warming."

above, left

A piece of mounted wood, turned this way and that, can lend itself to many treatments. Carole Bailey of Houston, Texas, works with one side and uses the curled heads of tree ferns to highlight the wood's direction. More curls appear at the base—looped ti and flax leaves around a bronze succulent. Pink-and-green anthuriums repeat the colors in the leaves.

above, right

New Zealand flax leaves (*Phormium tenax*) are bent to follow the bend of the wood in a design by Kitty Larkin of Menomonee Falls, Wisconsin. Orange lilies call attention to its hollowed-out interior.

opposite

The piece serves as a support for a swirl of fasciated mullein in a design by Marsha Webb of Sandy Springs, Georgia. Magnolia leaves and a hydrangea blossom, placed directly over the point of suspension, establish stability with no loss of rhythm.

above and opposite

A piece of polished wood, beautiful on both sides and hollowed out to accommodate an arranger's choice, was selected by Marie Cruse of Charlotte, North Carolina, and Gilda de Garcia of McAllen, Texas. Marie added the bold "wings" of a saguaro cactus, king protea, and palm fronds. Gilda, turning the wood, filled it with finger sponges on one end and white calla lilies on the other. Green anthuriums connect the two groupings.

opposite and right

A six-foot-tall piece of saguaro cactus caught the eye of Penny Decker of Ormond Beach, Florida, and Gilda de Garcia of McAllen, Texas. In Penny's design titled "Totem" (right), clipped palm fronds painted red fan out at the top and bottom of the skeletonized form, with fuzzy hanging She Kong heliconia repeating the red and adding another texture. Gilda carried the saguaro outside and placed it beside the highly textured bark of a pine tree. Hanging heliconia and New Zealand flax slash across the two trunks. Nestled in the pine needles are more saguaro, king proteas, anthuriums, and beehive gingers—a meeting of many worlds.

above
Elk antlers from Deen Day Sanders'
collection found an enthusiastic
reception with three arrangers. Katrina
Vollmer of Nashville, Indiana, saw a rack
for displaying the dramatic forms of red
ginger and coral peonies.

below
In "Northern Exposure," Claudia Chopp
of Wentzville, Missouri, arranged the
pair in a vase shape and filled it with
plant material suggestive of western
terrain—small sunflowers, cedar,
cryptomeria, holly, and cones.

opposite
Arabella Dane of Center Harbor, New
Hampshire, added deer antlers to the
elk ones, creating a tower of "natural
artifacts" punctuated by clementines,
apples, and leucodendron. A fatsia
leaf is at the base and monstera leaves
soar over the top. A title? The arranger
suggests "Horns of a Dilemma."

above

A circle of jade, one of the many treasures
in Deen Day Sanders' collection,
inspired two experienced arrangers.
Mary Jo Strawbridge of Merion Station,
Pennsylvania, calls attention to the colors
in the jade with a monochromatic design.
Strands and strands of bear grass are
braided together to create circles that
allow the jade to show through. Hydrangea
provides a variation in texture and color in
this tone-on-tone design.

above

The circle of jade reminded Gay Estes of Houston, Texas, of the artist Jasper Johns's Target series. She chose to embellish the jade in equally revolutionary style, with a tropical pod slinking over the top and a banana blossom balanced in the opening. The petals that follow the pod and drop down are from a heliconia blossom—new plant material for new art.

left
A sculpture of burnished copper is set aglow with coral peonies and arachnid orchids in a design by Kingslea Thomas of Houston, Texas. Looped ti and flax leaves underscore the darker tones.

opposite
Ruth Crocker of Cambridge, Massachusetts, saw a potential for contrast and rhythm in the same sculpture, adding succulents in palest green and connecting them with Flexi grass (*Ficinia fascicularis*).

Pauline Flynn of Port Huron, Michigan, began with an aluminum sculpture by Ken Schwartz. In the red design, she added a ball at the top and crackle glass and metal spikes. The spikes, candle holders to be inserted in plants, hold orange gerberas and the heads of *Allium schubertii.* In the blue design, another metal ball was added at the base and, behind it, a fan of battery-powered blue fiber-optic light. A mass of blue and white hydrangea seems to capture the light and send it out in loops of blue Lucite.

overleaf, left above

A glob of red plastic, once discarded but recognized and reclaimed by Deen Day Sanders, proved popular with three arrangers. Its melded lines are evident in the horizontal placement by Mary Jo Strawbridge of Merion Station, Pennsylvania. Mary Jo has emphasized the linear texture by attaching rows of sunflower petals to cardboard with double-sided tape, a technique called petalling. Green trachelium outlines the petals and jatropha stems continue the red of the plastic.

overleaf, left below

Placed at an angle so the curls will be evident, the plastic pierces a circle of wisteria vine in this composition by Deen Day Sanders of Duluth, Georgia. The thrust, color, and glossy quality are continued in red-and-yellow heliconias and red anthuriums on the other side of the circle, with a touch of lycopodium foliage for contrast. More circles appear in the container, all part of a design Deen calls, "Round and Round We Go."

overleaf, right

Katrina Vollmer of Nashville, Indiana, balanced the plastic on a two-part container and let the light shine through. Red-and-white lilies, white dendrobium orchids, a twist of white vine, and explosions of green cypress contribute to a very lively scene.

art meets art

Arrangers at the Memphis Flower Show
respond to the sometimes far-out art on
exhibit at the Dixon Gallery and Gardens.
Chicago's Show of Summer and
Houston's Florescence are also represented.

When is attendance at an art museum at its highest? When a new, much publicized exhibition opens? Possibly. But another occasion that dramatically increases attendance is a kind of festival of flowers—when the works of art in the museum's collection are complemented by flower arrangements. The first of these events in the United States, "Art in Bloom," was held more than three decades ago, in 1976, at the Museum of Fine Arts, Boston, the host city of the first World Flower Show to be held in the United States—in June of 2011.

The flowers-with-art formula proved a great success, serving both as a crowd-pleaser and a fund-raiser. Other museums across the country followed suit. The Wadsworth Atheneum in Hartford, Connecticut, launched "Fine Art and Flowers" in 1981. The San Francisco Auxiliary of the Fine Arts Museums first held "Bouquets to Art" in 1984. In *The Fine Art of Flower Arranging*, thirty museums and galleries that hold flower and art events on a regular basis were listed. We believe the number has increased since the book's publication.

A variation on the flowers-with-art theme is the competitive flower show in which arrangers complement works of art, their creations then being critiqued by a panel of judges. That was the case with the flower show held at the Dixon Gallery and Gardens in Memphis, Tennessee, and featured on the following pages. The Memphis Garden Club, in cooperation with the Dixon Gallery and Gardens, has hosted a Garden Club of America Major Flower Show in even years since 1984. The exhibition of art for the show is chosen by the Dixon curator, in cooperation with the flower show chairmen. In the 2008 show, all the art was three-dimensional—some freestanding; some wall hung; some suspended from the ceiling; some extending onto the gallery floor. Contemporary and edgy, the show featured works by ten artists with Memphis connections and was titled "M3D: On the Edge." The illustrated schedule was online, and exhibitors could choose their works of art as much as a year in advance—and begin thinking.

Thinking, according to arrangers who enter either flowers-and-art events or art-related flower shows, is the best part. They relish the challenge of researching the work of art in depth, something few museum visitors make time for, and taking the next step—selecting design elements in the art that they can represent in their composition. The goal is to communicate to museum visitors what the arranger saw

page 136

A bronze sculpture, titled *Torso*, by artist Carroll Todd led arranger Katie Olsen of Winnetka, Illinois, to focus on the negative space around the form. Katie says, "I flattened the space by using wooden cutouts (carried in my suitcase), which I connected to each other and to the pedestal top at the show." The reverse silhouette is topped with hydrangea flowerets and pink mink proteas. The snake grass looping over the top and the string of succulent pearls dropping down the front add movement to a voluptuous design.

opposite

The Houston, Texas, team of Carole Bailey and Mariane Brewster approached a class in the 2008 Memphis Flower Show with all the fervor the class titled "Whirl" required. They interpreted artist Brian Russell's cast glass and steel sculpture with the luminous forms of yellow anthuriums on the ends of green stemlike tubes. A bundle of equisetum reflects the strength and slant of the base in Russell's design.

in the artwork. Visitors come in record numbers to see the flowers, and linger longer in front of a work of art than they would otherwise. Most important, they see what the arranger—with a year to study the art—saw. It's a formula that pleases arrangers, museums, and visitors.

The Garden Club of Houston and the River Oaks Garden Club host a Garden Club of America Major Flower Show at the Museum of Fine Arts, Houston, in odd years—alternating with the Memphis show. Sandy Patterson's design on page 156 complements an Abstract Expressionist painting by Hans Hofmann in the permanent collection of the MFA Houston.

Even nonmuseum shows take advantage of the synergy that is created between art and interpretive flower arrangements. Elvira Butz's design on page 157 was featured in "Tapestries," the 2008 "Show of Summer" held at the Chicago Botanic Garden, a Garden Club of America Major Flower Show sponsored by five area garden clubs.

Fine art, which is permanent, meets the ephemeral art of flower arranging on the following pages.

opposite, above
Cary Lide of Atlanta, Georgia, chose a sculpture by Carroll Todd titled *Lost in the Woods*. "And," in Cary's words, "that is what I felt for about six months. I finally settled on contrast rather than replication, using a container of wood that could be manipulated into different shapes." The bronze ball inside Todd's sculpture is represented by a mass of orange lilies in Cary's design.

opposite, below
Brian Russell is a master of forged metals and cast glass, exploring the nature of light and form. Here, Ruth Crocker of Cambridge, Massachusetts, explores light and form with calla lilies following the form of the sculpture and roses supplying the light. A grid of red-twig dogwood holds the nestlike form, a reference to the sculpture's title, *Large Hemisphere 41: Nest*.

left
The neon sign is only one part of the work of art that Carol McDonald and Kristin Brown of Monroe, Louisiana, chose to interpret. Not showing is the skeleton of a tree hung from the ceiling, parallel to the floor. Carol says they chose the work by Terry Jones "because of the audaciousness in the simplicity of 'the hanging tree' with the message 'Hurry' in neon." Carol, who already owned the sculpture in the design, and Kristin placed a blue neon light between the two parts and painted the stamen of a white anthurium neon blue. The bare tree, suspended by twisted airplane wire, is represented by jagged sticks behind the sculpture and a coil of lead at the front.

above

In artist Maysey Craddock's *2 Sisters,* two antique children's hoop skirts are hung upside down, one inside the other. "It was clear from the beginning," arranger Lee LaPointe of Vero Beach, Florida, reports, "that the complementary interpretation must be a hanging design." A stick-and-hoop toy provided the framework, suggesting the play of two young sisters in an earlier era. A beaded heart was attached by a swivel, allowing it to whirl as the skirts once did. Palm fiber was bleached, dried, and stretched to suggest dress fabric; basket-weaving material was soaked in tea to darken it, then woven through the heart. When the heart turns, two small, heart-shaped red anthuriums can be seen on the opposite side. The interpretation, Lee said, evolved to be about "sisterly love and the ties that bind and enmesh us all in our ancestry."

above, left

In a sculpture titled *The Bloom of Your Words Touched Me*, artist Maysey Craddock deconstructed a typewriter and used the keys to create a flower. Arranger Lida Bross of Memphis, Tennessee, interpreted Craddock's composition with red anthuriums, tips of red stem dogwood, and pincushion proteas. Calla lilies, spray-painted red, and red-stem dogwood branches reach down the side of the white pedestal.

above, right

Helen Goddard of South Dartmouth, Massachusetts, looked at a metal-and-fabric sculpture by Maysey Craddock and saw a parallel design. The threads that hang down are suggested by a row of costus stems, wrapped for emphasis but also to hold sprays of phalaenopsis orchids that, in turn, echo the sweep of the fabric. Black sticks in a pavéd ball of white carnations recall the spokes of the wheel, and galax leaves have the visual weight and rotation of the hub.

overleaf, left

Artist Greely Myatt's eight-foot-tall *Scrub Board* was made from old broom handles. Claudia Lummis and Trish Chambers of Houston, Texas, picked up on the recycling theme and took it a step further. Their design consists of an old breadboard, a washtub, and a "scrub board" made of old fencing material and bamboo. The painted bamboo picks up the colors of the broom handles. The tub is filled with washday suds—hydrangea blossoms and mini calla lilies.

overleaf, right

The oval of polished cedar in the corner is part of Greeley Myatt's sculpture *A Muse*. The "message" the muse is sending to the oval is interpreted by Deborah Tipton of Memphis, Tennessee, in orange and black ribbons swirling through a wooden grid. Artichokes recall the sculpture's dark color and multilayered texture, while the orange in the construction is reflected in birds-of-paradise.

above
Artist Greely Myatt obviously likes thought bubbles. This one is composed of recycled cookie tins and titled *Roulette*. Arranger Pat Schnack of Honolulu, Hawaii, found a burned-out bicycle wheel in her neighborhood and put it to use on the roulette theme. The Plexiglas support was recycled from another show. Anthuriums and billy balls (*Craspedia* sp.) set the wheel in motion and reflect the colors of the wall installation.

opposite
Greely Myatt continues his fondness for thought bubbles and recycling in this wall sculpture titled *Talking Trio*. The speech balloons were crafted from reclaimed wood and steel, one covered in vintage ceiling tile—and a zipper; one with the measuring grid from an old paper cutter; and two with painted plywood. Arranger Ingrid Kelly of Houston, Texas, set out to use only recycled material. She chose a skirt marker to elevate her design and for its references to the colors

and material on the wall. Galvanized hardware cloth, a repeat of the grid pattern, was shaped to represent the main thought bubble with a descending row of vintage Christmas light-bulbs as the directional. The resulting defined space was filled with a feast of color, form, and texture—anthuriums, bromeliad blossoms, pincushion protea, peppers, bird's nest fern, galax leaves, and—most intriguing—the inflorescence of the bottle plant (*Jatropha podagrica*).

opposite

Greely Myatt's work, with its wit and style, enchanted any number of arrangers and visitors at the Memphis Flower Show. This piece was titled *The Fool with an Idea or Two*. The two arrangers who tackled it—Gay Estes, of Houston, Texas, and Linda Holden, of Staunton, Virginia—had many ideas. The first was to build a Cubist form in the same white, black, and ocher of the figure in the wall art. To this they added electrical wire, a plug, and "lightbulbs"—actually salt shakers from a craft store—filled with bullion wire and flowers. Pincushion proteas help electrify the scene.

right

Myatt is at work again in this life-size sculpture of carved and painted polystyrene titled *A Formal Arrangement*. This work of art remained unclaimed after most of the other works in the flower show schedule had been snapped up by enthusiastic arrangers. Two committee members, Ruthie Bowlin and Mary Robinson of Memphis, Tennessee, agreed to tackle it. The container on the bottom supports a "cypress root, thick as a tree trunk, misshapen, bristly, irresistible," that was spotted in a New York flower shop by Ruthie five years before the show. It came home to await its moment. In the design, the root supports an armature of chicken wire, bundled willow, and water tubes. The tubes, in turn, are filled with hundreds of pink anthuriums and painted grasses. The result has all the drama of prom night.

At the Memphis Flower Show, the walls of one gallery were filled with commanding silhouettes in cut black felt by artist Allison Smith. The title of the class that featured the works was "Felt Not Seen."

right

Little Cowboy by Allison Smith intrigued Mary Lynn Majors and Martha McClellan of Knoxville, Tennessee, and appealed to their love of Western art. The trail of the components tells a tale of arranger resourcefulness. The fence post and horseshoes came from a farm in Knoxville, the barbed wire from a ranch in Montana. The big birds-of-paradise (*Strelitzia nicolai*), which look more ominous than the Little Cowboy's guns, were ordered weeks in advance. Their white blossoms were removed and the bracts rubbed with olive oil. The strelitzia stems were sprayed with black paint, then dusted with silvery blue eye shadow. At the base is a campfire of bromeliad blossoms, pincushion protea, and an array of prickly, sculptural cacti. The bromeliad blossoms were dipped in Plasti Dip to keep them pristine, a tip picked up in Bliss Clark's Random Resources column in *GCA by Design*.

opposite

Two Connecticut arrangers, Ellen Avellino of Greenwich and Peggy Moore of Fairfield, responded to Smith's *Walls Have Ears*. In the bent form, they saw a distressed woman whose words had come back to haunt her—represented by the scolding bird and all the ears on the wall. They exaggerated the ear forms with wooden cutouts covered in black and flesh-colored yarn to extend the craft quality of Smith's work. Anthuriums and the rhythmic placement of the ears represent the movement of gossip. Their statement of intent: "Yes, walls have ears, and you won't believe what we just heard!"

overleaf, left

The shapely contours of *Donkey Woman* by Smith are captured in the container used by two Memphis, Tennessee, arrangers, Mary Carr and Mary Ellis. A close look reveals that the container is composed of two flowerpots, one inverted, the two forms connected at the "waist" by a belt that harks back to the harness the figure is holding. Pincushion proteas, painted black with red tips, and balls of moss complete the torso while pussy willow branches and wrapped grass provide the "limbs." White chrysanthemums supply the sparkle implied by the stars over the donkey head.

overleaf, right

There's a lot going on in this felt sculpture by Smith, which is simply titled *Dog*. Bel Lamb of Beaumont, Texas, has woven references from the different parts into her rhythmic three-part design. The frenzied cat in midflight is represented in a ball of curly willow and hypericum berries suspended at the end of a wire. The apple in the pig's mouth appears on a plate in the arrangement, accented by an orange lily and surrounded by black flexible flower holders. According to Bel, who has four dogs, "The dog's tail was my favorite component. I used sago palm, painted red, for wag appeal."

Class II
Felt Not Seen

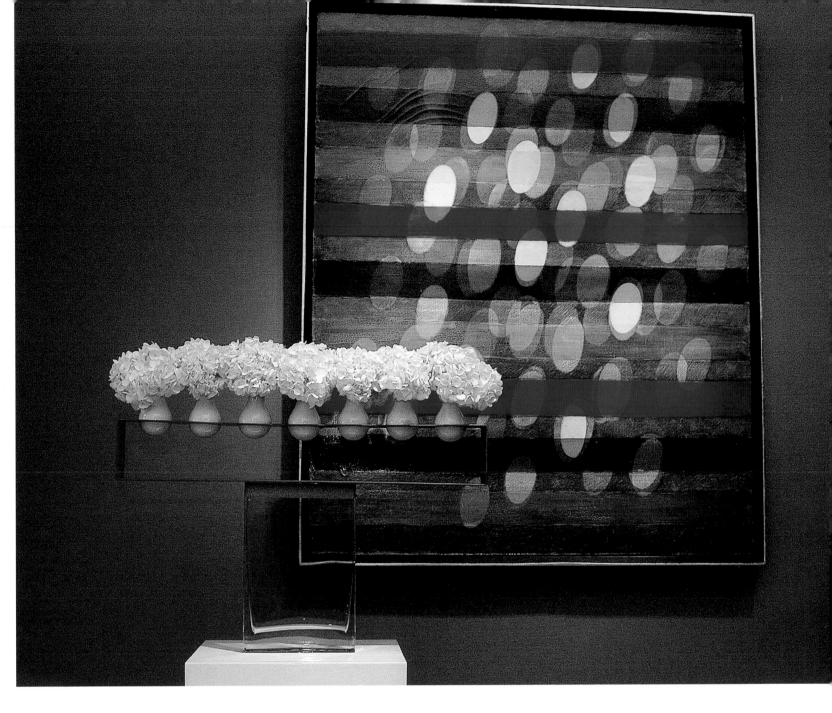

opposite

Three minds may be better than one when it comes to the table classes at the Memphis Flower Show, and ideas certainly flew when three Memphis arrangers—Dabney Coors, Pam McFarland, and Sissy Pettit—teamed up to interpret Ted Faiers' *The Flying Salesman.* Over the course of a year, they worked on dozens of details that relate to the painting, and a viewer could spend the better part of an hour finding and appreciating each one. Dominant in the design is the table, which they had constructed. "It's level," Dabney points out, "like the frame of the painting, but is supported by twisted wooden rope legs that are askew, or, as we say in the

South, 'woppy-jawed,' like the ropes in the painting."

The table covering is burlap, the color of the man's suit, with a stripe across it. The hemp rug is the color of the sky, and the triangular place mat echoes the chevron in the painting. A salesman's attaché case and vintage goggles sit on the floor. "The stylized eye in the arrangement," Dabney explains, "is created of Nikko blue hydrangea blossoms and a painted coconut. It underscores the painting's focal point—the salesman's eyeglasses and bowler hat." There's more, but even with the myriad details, the spare quality of the painting is preserved.

above

In the 2006 Memphis Flower Show, Maryjo Garre of Barrington, Illinois, chose a painting by Burton Callicott titled *Sunlight on Stripes.* Where the artist saw sunlight, Maryjo saw lightbulbs and asked her husband, Sandy, if he could cut the metal ends off bulbs so she could put water in them. A hacksaw was the tool of choice. She searched for a votive candleholder with many openings and found this one, which she painted red, at Target. Yellow food coloring in a glass container of water and a stripe of masking tape painted blue echo the yellow and blue in the painting. White hydrangea blossoms turned on the power in a class titled "Light, Line, and Laughter."

Sandra Patterson of Portola Valley, California, chose *Summer Over the Land,* an oil painting by Abstract Expressionist Hans Hofmann when she entered "Florescence Cosmos," the 2007 flower show held at the Museum of Fine Arts, Houston. The brushstrokes in the gestural painting appealed to her. She said, "Sweeping his brush boldly across the painting's surface, Hofmann achieves incredible movement as colors come crashing together. I tried to capture the strong brushwork and movement by painting dried phormium leaves and strips of bamboo with brushes (and my fingers) in varying shades of orange and pink acrylic and then sweeping them in and out of the sinuous Sogetsu ikebana container. Hofmann's accents in yellow and rust are reflected in curving and swooping anthuriums. The viewer, can look through to the painting and, I hope, see what I saw."

The 2008 "Show of Summer," held at the Chicago Botanic Garden, took as its theme "Tapestry, the Interwoven World." Elvira Butz of Winnetka, Illinois, entered a class titled "The Fabric of Time," in which the arranger was to supply the fabric to be complemented. Years ago, Elvira studied various tribes and their customs in Irian Jaya, the western part of Papua, New Guinea. While she was there, two pieces of bark cloth were presented to her in a special ceremony; she combined the two in a frame as the basis for this design. The ceremonial gourds at the base of the design are also from Irian Jaya, while the giant bean pods (*Entada gigas*) were found in Madagascar over twenty years ago. Banana blossoms, celosia, and banksia proteas are among the exotic offerings at the base of the design. The bark cloth and other components are a reference, Elvira explains, to ritual objects offered to venerable ancestors and spirits in ceremonies linking the natural and supernatural worlds in the tribal societies.

6

turning the tables

The form, not the function, of plates,
glasses, and other dining components
is the creative driver behind exhibition tables.
These are not typical dinner tables, but with
a little focus, the art in this flower show class
can become crystal clear.

page 158
American artist Alexander Calder inspired this exhibition-style table with plates and cups suitable for a picnic. Marsha Webb of Sandy Springs, Georgia, studied the Calder Foundation website and, she said, "tried to use shapes that reflected the essence of his work. Many of his mobiles, stabiles, and also some lithographs feature similar forms, including *Big Bird,* 1937, *Elephant,* 1936, and *Triple Gong,* 1951." The "stabile" for Marsha's table setting is fashioned from foam board with the top piece raised and supported by perpendicular pieces, creating depth and Calderesque spaces in a design Marsha calls "Calder's Cauldron." Hydrangea blossoms, sea oats, and ting ting applied to the panel and painted Calder red provide a change in texture, as do the palm fronds and the orange-red gerbera. Calder was once asked in an interview how he knew when it was time to stop working in his studio. He replied, "When it's time for dinner."

Near the end of the last section, we saw an art-inspired "functional table setting." The definition of a functional table setting is, in flower show parlance, simply a table set for the actual service of food. In the picture on page 154, in addition to the components referencing the aerialist in the painting, a plate, glass, and napkin are placed familiarly on the surface of a table.

By contrast, designers of "exhibition table settings" avoid functionality and almost literally topple the tables, turning them on edge, possibly even upside down. The components that would be used in dining—glasses, plates, napkins—are still employed, but for their design qualities alone. A red plate mounted on edge is still a familiar piece of dining equipment, but now the focus is on its round form and bold color—its design rather than its function.

Exhibition table settings must include plant material, either fresh or dried, but the material need not be in a conventional flower arrangement. It may be placed wherever the arranger feels it best serves design purposes.

Looking at the designs on the next few pages, readers of this book might well feel—as Dorothy did in The Wizard of Oz—that we're not in Kansas anymore. Certainly not in the familiar territory of setting the table for dinner, but a closer look will reveal that we are not far from the flowers-and-art concept seen in the preceding chapter. There, arrangers complemented works of art with their own floral designs. Here, arrangers often take inspiration from artists and incorporate their signature styles into three-dimensional designs that include the familiar components of the dinner table.

For example, on page 158, Marsha Webb creates a structure reminiscent of a stabile by the American artist Alexander Calder as the staging for her components. Just as Calder sculptures are frequently placed outdoors, so the casual components of this table setting suggest alfresco dining or a picnic. Deanna Mozzochi takes her inspiration from Piet Mondrian, with primary colors and a geometrical frame to reference the grid pattern so closely identified with the Dutch artist (page 162).

In the flower show "Land of Oz" of exhibition table settings, it may help to see them as window or display art. Think of the windows on New York's Fifth Avenue that stop pedestrians in their tracks—delighting them with their wit and innovation or making them shake their heads in disbelief. Gene Moore is credited with bringing art to the windows of Fifth Avenue, especially Tiffany and Company's five little windows.

"Eating from Every Angle" is the title Deanna Mozzochi of Westbrook, Connecticut, has given this exhibition table setting. A red Plexiglas stand by artist Joy Parker provides the framework for the red, black, and white dining components. Painted flax leaves move out from the cluster of red gerberas and slice through the half circle in the red sculpture. Clipped, painted palm fronds echo the angles on the right. A single red gerbera rests at the base of a champagne glass, a bold black form of rounded and straight lines.

For almost half a century—at Tiffany for thirty-nine years and for Bonwit Teller, Bergdorf Goodman, and I. Miller before that—Moore transformed the storefront window from a crowded display space to a recessed work of art. He enlisted artists like Robert Rauschenberg to provide backdrop paintings and gave Jasper Johns his first public exhibition as part of a Bonwit Teller window display. It is in this same spirit that arrangers entering exhibition table classes approach their assignments—raising the display of dinnerware to an art form. As Gay Estes wrote in the Spring 1996 issue of *The Flower Arranging Study Group Newsletter* (now *GCA by Design*): "Clearly, table classes are no tea parties for sissies! They are literally frozen tableaux, still lifes—hinting at hospitality. They are a vehicle for the clever and disciplined arranger. Best of all, tables are fun! Let the visual feast continue!"

opposite

Arranger Deanna Mozzochi of Westbrook, Connecticut, took her inspiration for an exhibition-style table from Piet Mondrian, the Dutch artist famous for his grid-based abstract paintings with blocks of primary colors. In a wooden frame by Carol Ziegler, Dee has inserted red, yellow, blue, and white plastic boxes to represent the colors in Mondrian's *Composition with Red, Blue, and Yellow,* 1921. The components are raised off the table surface and mounted in a display- or exhibition-style position. Red, blue, and yellow plates continue the blocks of color, while dried and painted palmetto leaves offer a change in texture and even suggest pleated napkins. A single yellow gerbera is featured in Dee's composition, which she titles "Munch with Mondrian" or, alternatively, "Primary Places."

right

The color red dances through this design by Jackie Payne of Alpharetta, Georgia. Beginning with the grouping at the base—plate, candles, and mat—through the napkin, roses, and bromeliad blossoms to the inverted glass at the top, the composition lives up to its title, "Red Hot Time." The metal sculpture by Ken Schwartz contributes to the fast-paced movement and reflects the blue of the Fitz and Floyd plate with its morning-glory design.

left
A metal stand elevates and holds a wall sconce for votive candles. Deanna Mozzochi, of Westbrook, Connecticut, has added wooden circles in black and red, underscoring the form of the sconce and the black-and-white plates. Red gerberas with black centers continue the repetition, while painted, sharply tapered palmetto fronds echo the stems of the champagne glasses.

opposite
Curves dominate this dramatic exhibition table setting by Marsha Webb of Sandy Springs, Georgia, which features plant material related to food. The curvaceous forms that move from bottom to top in the design are Brussels sprout stalks—after the sprouts have been removed. The black form that frames one anthurium blossom is a gourd. A lime-green vase echoes the anthuriums and balances the composition.

overleaf, left
Julie Lapham of Southborough, Massachusetts, named this exhibition table setting "Monkey Fanfare." Fans, large and small, move in and out and around two malachite plates and a goblet, carafe, and cup and saucer. A napkin the color of the fans drapes over a table runner of darkest green, echoing the napkin near the large plate. But it is the decorated ceramic monkey who steals the show. Atop his head he balances an arrangement of *Gibbaeum* sp., a green succulent, and the curled gray leaves of *Cecropia peltata*.

overleaf, right
Hearts, large and small, blue and yellow, unite this exhibition table setting by Betty Grimes of Hiawassee, Georgia. A white frame provides spaces to be filled—with yellow fabric, blue glasses, and wicker umbrellas brimming with blue hydrangea blossoms. A heart-shaped plate against a yellow charger balances the two plates mounted on the yellow panel.

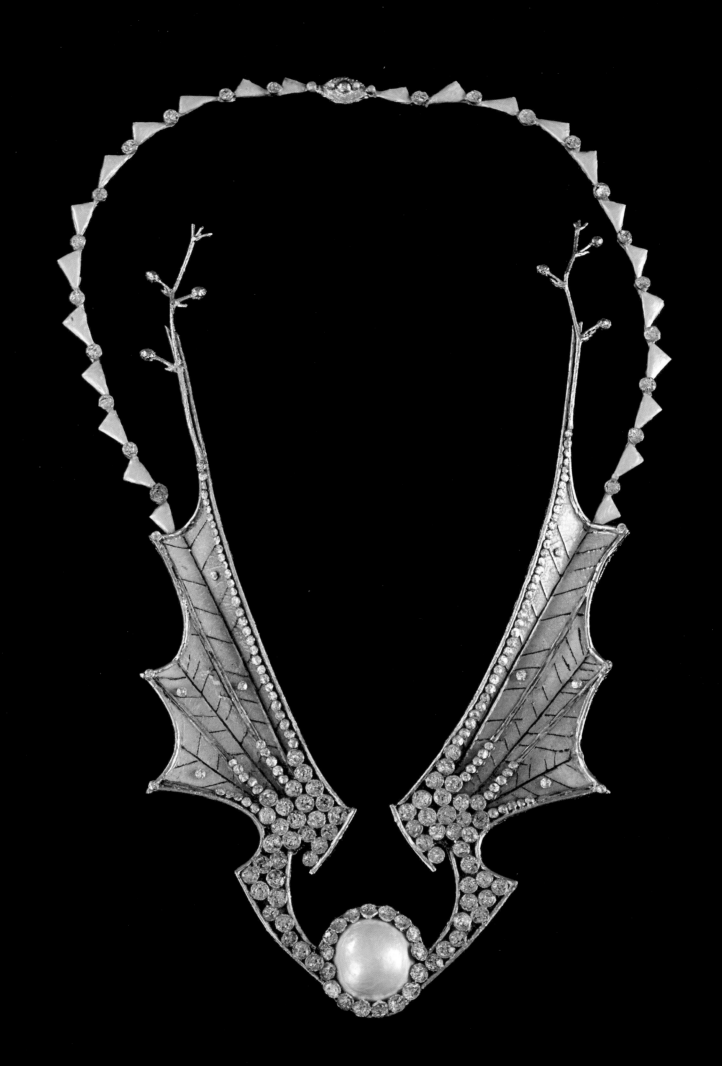

7

nature's adornments

With a Midas touch, arrangers turn beans and seeds, pods and vines into jewelry that a queen—or an Academy Award winner— might envy.

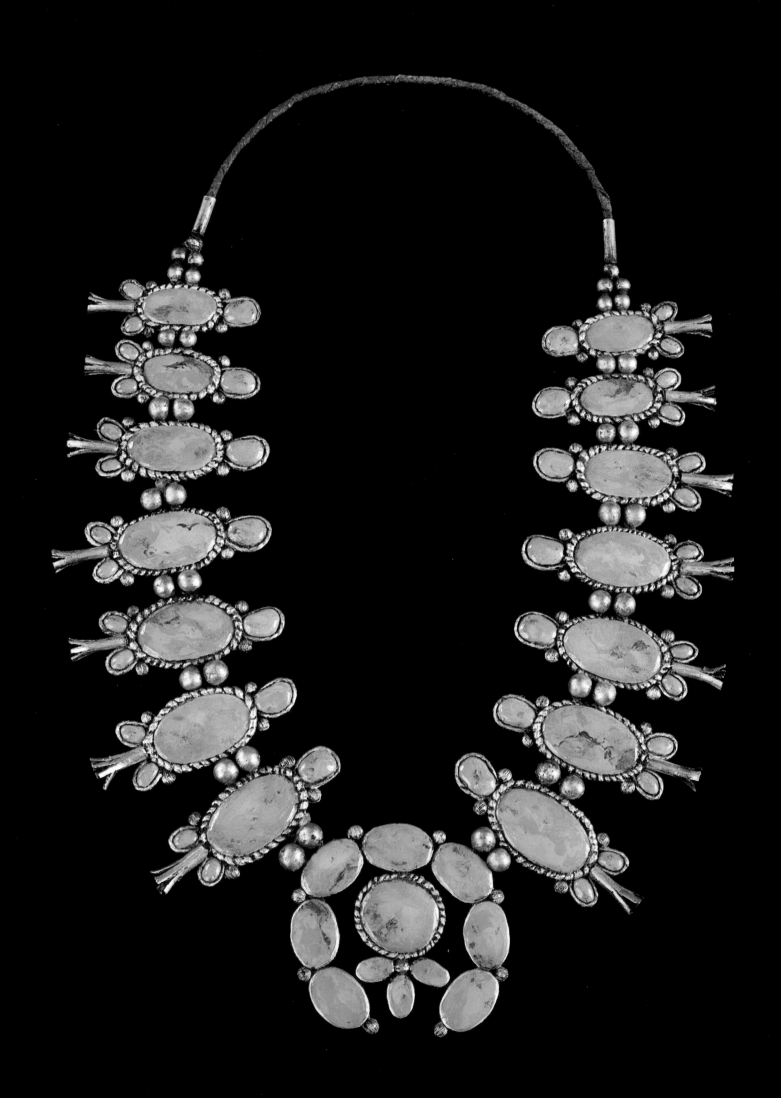

opposite
A class in the 2005 Philadelphia Flower Show called for "a necklace inspired by the Wild West." Bel Lamb of Beaumont, Texas, took up that challenge. In her research, she came across a squash-blossom necklace in a book of Native American jewelry. She was off and carving and sanding and painting. The larger pieces of turquoise in the necklace are cut from a gourd with a band saw, then sanded, according to Bel, "on this great little craft belt sander I purchased at a hardware store. Next, I hand sanded and then painted each piece and sprinkled them with copper paint pigment to create veining. Tons of coats of clear nail polish give depth." Lima and navy beans were used for the smaller pieces of turquoise and nandina berries for the silver beads.

Coriander seeds form the fluting around the turquoise pieces and split cane, pried open, decorates the ends. The necklace thong is made from bark.

Bel adds, "The other important component of this piece is the silver. I used a silver Krylon paint pen, but have found that by rubbing raw umber acrylic paint over the silver, you get an aged appearance."

above
Turquoise is the focus of this necklace, too, but this time the underlying plant material is a shiitake mushroom. Connie Teuscher of Beaumont, Texas, added "feathers" made from wild senna leaves (*Cassia alata*) and a chain woven from Spanish moss (*Tillandsia usneodes*). "Texas Power" was the title of the class.

overleaf, left top
Alice Farley is a regular exhibitor in the jewelry classes at her hometown's world-famous event, the Philadelphia Flower Show. This was her entry in a class that called for "jewelry to be worn by a belly dancer," and here's how she approached it: "I wanted something that both revealed and concealed. I felt the design should feel reflective, gossamer, fragile, and work with a costume that might include veils. And I felt it should grade in weight and scale as it moved away from the neck. Since all jewelry designs for the Philadelphia Flower Show must function as jewelry (i.e., you should be able to pick it up and apply it to the body), my choice of extremely fragile pine needles and tiny seeds was problematic. Although it is now quite fragile, as a freshly minted piece it was remarkably sturdy."

overleaf, left bottom
Farley has a distinguished history of creating finely detailed pieces, so when the schedule called for a bolder "Pre-Columbian" style, she felt stumped. But not for long. She researched what features would make a piece recognizably Mayan or Incan. "I wanted my piece to appear to be hammered gold," Alice explains, "so I looked for material with a texture that was bold enough to appear through an overlay of gold leaf. Maple samaras fit the bill, as did milkweed pods and London plane tree fruits. I think the simplicity of a single finish—gold leaf—makes the piece appear both Pre-Columbian and sleekly modern. It's a necklace I would enjoy wearing!"

overleaf, right
"Southern Beauty," a class in a River Oaks Garden Club flower show in Houston, asked arrangers to embellish "a lady's hand mirror for her dressing table." Carole Bailey responded with craftmanship to rival the metalworking techniques of repoussé and chasing. Acorns rotate around a basket filled with flower forms, including poppy seed heads. Caracalla bean pods (*Vigna caracalla*) swirl up the handle, and jasmine vine defines the edges.

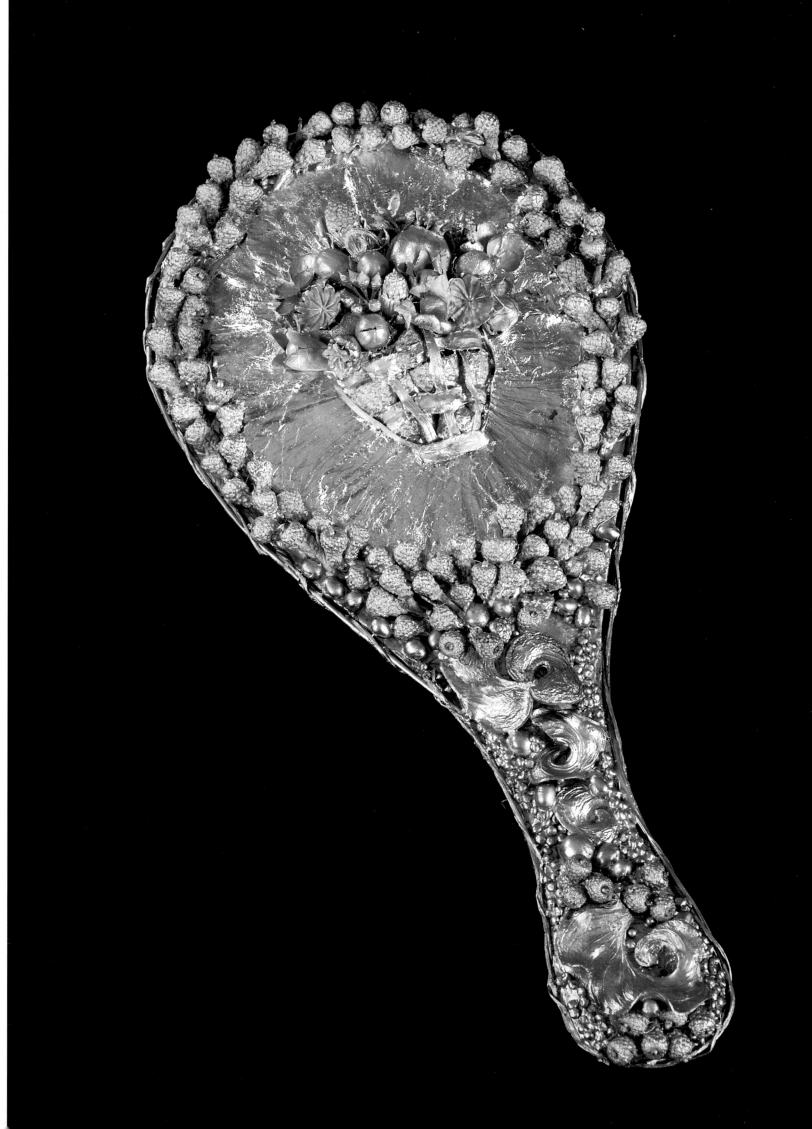

above

This tiara by Carole Bailey of Houston, Texas, was an entry in the 2007 Florescence Flower Show held at the Museum of Fine Arts, Houston. The large pearls are Texas buckeye (*Aescules glabra* var. *arguta*) in "windows" of seedpods from *Brachychiton bidwillii,* a shrub from Australia known as Little Kurrajong. The small pearls, crape myrtle seeds (*Lagerstoemia indica*), drop from tendrils of coral vine (*Antigonon leptopus*). A poppy seed head anchors the front, and wheat adds detail to the band.

opposite

The fashion of including jewelry classes in flower shows reached the show held at the New Orleans Museum of Art in 2005. Melinda Earle of Naples, Florida, entered this design in a class asking for a crown or tiara for Mardi Gras. With laurel oak, soybeans, slash pine, almonds, and Norfolk Island pine, she created a headpiece worthy of a Mardi Gras queen. In fact, she won the Rose Naumen Award and Ms. Naumen, a longtime museum supporter, said it reminded her of one she had worn to a Mardi Gras ball.

marvelous masses

The style may change—from period to traditional to line-mass—but the love of an abundance of flowers remains strong. American arrangers embrace the modern mass and its innovative possibilities.

While American flower arrangers are eager to learn about and put into practice the latest trends and innovations, there continues to exist a respect, even a fondness, for what is known as the traditional mass arrangement. The closed silhouette of the traditional mass stems from a Western flower arranging ethos that has its roots in gardening and showcasing the bounty of nature. By contrast, the Eastern—Japanese or ikebana—tradition evolved from early religious offerings, focusing on the branches and buds of growing plants and the open silhouette created by them.

The traditional mass, as it has been known since the early part of the twentieth century, follows hundreds of years of other Western "mass styles"—most notably the Dutch and Flemish Baroque, in which each horticultural specimen is showcased; French Rococo, with a curvaceous yet delicate airiness; Georgian, where the emphasis is on harmony; Federal, with a formal symmetry suggesting the Neoclassical; and Victorian—the ultimate in showing off the bounty of the garden, tightly massed mounds of blossoms.

America's own history of flower arranging probably began with gatherings from the meadows or a handful of blossoms grown from seeds carried from the old country. When wealth replaced subsistence in such cities as Charleston, South Carolina; Williamsburg, Virginia; Philadelphia, Pennsylvania; New York City; Newport, Rhode Island; and Boston, Massachusetts, European fashions were adapted for the halls and dining rooms of the grandest homes.

This was largely the case in America for three hundred years, until the early twentieth century. Then the tightly packed masses of the Victorian era gave way to a somewhat more open and flexible style called a traditional mass. The flexibility meant that any one arrangement might have elements of earlier period styles and at the same time move toward what we now consider a more contemporary look. This opportunity for variation, this flexibility, probably accounts for its popularity over the ensuing hundred years. It is, at a very basic level, a style that resonates with the garden lover in the American public, a public that delights in an abundance of flowers formally arranged.

There are places and occasions where a traditional mass seems the best, even the only choice. A beautiful home with elegant period furniture is certainly one of these, and on the following pages beautiful settings are complemented by equally beautiful arrangements. After the examples of traditional mass designs, we will see

page 178
Light shines through a vase covered in skeletonized leaves of magnolia, held in place with randomly wrapped silver bullion wire. More of the leaves appear with dozens of hybrid tea roses (*Rosa* 'Voodoo') in this contemporary mass design by Tasha Tobin of Akron, Ohio. Strips of chair caning swirl around the sphere, setting the whole in rotation.

opposite
For this mass design with one material, Jackie Payne of Alpharetta, Georgia, filled a copper container with *Magnolia grandiflora* flowers and foliage. Porcelain magnolias with warblers, by Royal Worcester, flank the arrangement; the Sanders garden is reflected in the mirror.

the linear influence of ikebana, with line-mass (also called massed-line) designs, some
with a distinctly contemporary feel.

Perhaps the greatest revolution in mass arrangements in America has been the
adoption of the European style known as modern mass. Many American designers
were first introduced to this style by Paola Berger of Italy, through demonstrations
and the groundbreaking book she did with Loli Marsano, *Scultura Floreale*. Other
Italian designers—Gin Raboudi, Liliana Ghisalberti, Carla Barbaglia, and Guisi Ferrari
Cielo, as well as Danielle Espinasse of Paris—reinforced the modern mass message for
participants in Flower Arranging Study Group workshops.

A modern mass is characterized by a limited variety of plant material, with
a mass of one kind next to a mass of a contrasting texture; often, contemporary
techniques such as looping are included. Ingrid Kelly's design on page 197, illustrates
these points.

In this chapter, devoted to marvelous masses, mass ultimately encompasses all
designs using an abundance of plant material, so we close with Marty Van Allen's two
innovative designs on pages 201 and 203—one using hundreds of calla lilies in blocks
of pink, white, black, yellow, lavender, and burgundy; the other creating a tapestry of
textures using only green.

right

Charlyne Harrison of Atlanta, Georgia, chose roses, freesias, carnations, and alstromeria in pinks and whites to complement the young lady in the painting, a portrait of Jeanne Kieffer by American artist John Singer Sargent, commissioned in 1879. White candlesticks repeat the color and textural quality of the decorated vase. The three are displayed on an American chest from the Federal period, 1775–1830.

opposite

Two pink Herend vases suggested the color palette for this mass arrangement by Jackie Payne of Alpharetta, Georgia. She has filled a Victorian vase of burnished copper with azaleas, roses, larkspur, nandina blossoms, ferns, and eucalyptus. Vases and arrangement are reflected in a hand-carved Adam mirror, made in Scotland in 1747. It is one of a pair that hung in the Metropolitan Museum of Art for a number of years; the pair now graces the solarium of Deen Day Sanders' home in Duluth, Georgia.

overleaf, left
Grand mass arrangements in the symmetrical Federal style are the trademark of Dr. Felton Norwood of Atlanta, Georgia. Here he combines roses, gerberas, irises, lilies, snapdragons, delphiniums, proteas, and flowering quince in a tour de force of pinks and reds, blues and purples, greens and whites. Two classical figures hold the mass aloft.

overleaf, right
In *The Fine Art of Flower Arranging*, the Victorian style of flower arranging is described as follows: "Flower arrangement in this period reflected a love of the color, forms, and personalities of plants. Specimens with bizarre markings were favored as they were in Dutch paintings, but instead of setting each flower apart, the Victorian arranger massed the blossoms together, creating an overall effect suggesting rich embroidery."

"Rich embroidery" could certainly describe this mass arrangement by Kathy Rainer of Atlanta, Georgia. With a palette designed to excite—reds and pinks, peaches and corals, yellows and greens, Kathy has stitched a tapestry with five varieties of roses, two kinds of dahlias, lilies, even a flowering cabbage. The rounded silhouette, the antique silver container, and the delight in nature's offerings all contribute to the Victorian feel.

opposite
A formal pedestal and urn hold an explosion of yellows in this mass arrangement that is reminiscent of the harmonious Georgian style. Lucinda Seale of Jasper, Texas, has blended lilies and tulips in clear yellow with irises, gerberas, orchids, and asters in deeper and lighter hues. Foliage, in a variety of textures, adds interest and extends over the rim of the urn to unite the two components. The whole forms an ideal complement to this garden terrace.

above
The flowers in artist Daniel Ridgway Knight's (1839–1924) painting, *Fleurs des Champs,* seem to move out of the frame and into Charlyne Harrison's airy, French-style mass arrangement. A French Empire urn holds a selection of roses, hydrangea, larkspur, yarrow, nandina, and winter honeysuckle foliage gathered by Charlyne and her husband, Dr. John Harrison, in their garden. Green chrysanthemums from the market reflect the green in the painting.

right

Pat Hartrampf of Atlanta, Georgia, gives the mass arrangement a contemporary feel in this design that features lilacs, hydrangea, phalaenopsis orchids, roses, and tuberoses, among others. She lined a glass-and-silver cylinder with moss, bringing the greens of the arrangement into the container. Grouping, favored by the modern mass style, is evident in the bananas that reach over the rim and the cluster of mahonia blossoms just above them. The blue of hyacinths electrifies the design.

opposite

A breakfast room, already welcoming with yellow walls and accents of blue, is beautifully complemented with this arrangement by Betty Grimes of Hiawassee, Georgia. Blue hydrangea, yellow freesias, button mums, yarrow, even miniature pineapples that reiterate the hospitality theme, are combined in an English Spode terrine. Matching tea service and napkins await the next guest. Loops of wood, treated French blue, add a contemporary touch to the arrangement and call attention to the antique porcelain platter and plates on the wall. Chinese export, they were made for the English market and bear British coats of arms or crests.

opposite
Pat Setzer of Columbia, South Carolina, leads us into a Southern garden with a mass arrangement of foliage likely to be found there—magnolia, hens and chicks (*Sempervivum* sp.), hosta, holly, aspidistra, and gardenia. Blossoms—*Magnolia grandiflora*, Lenten rose (*Hellebore* sp.), sparkleberry (*Vaccinium arboreum*)—move the eye through the design. The cool, crisp arrangement sits atop a lead-colored birdbath.

left
An aluminum sculpture in the form of a treble clef supports a creative mass design of stargazer lilies, pink anthuriums, and magenta dendrobium orchids with pink torch ginger carrying the high notes. Margaret Kirkpatrick of Longwood, Florida, has assembled this chorus with foxtail asparagus, leather leaf, and palm foliage supporting the bright performers.

overleaf, left
Garden steps seem the perfect setting for this line-mass design by Gretchen Riley of Haverford, Pennsylvania. Bells of Ireland begin a line that travels through the design, joined by ascending coral peonies and hosta leaves. Repetition—in the bells' florets, the placement of the peonies, and the lines of the container—is continued in the stone steps.

overleaf, right
The orange of the container spoke loud and clear to Leslie Purple of Wyndmoor, Pennsylvania. In this line-mass design, orange gerberas establish a bold path that is extended, top and bottom, by heliconia blossoms and bells of Ireland. Looped and variegated ti leaves (*Cordyline* sp.) and loops of bear grass create spatial interest.

opposite
A strong line, an abundance of material, and a contemporary feel combine in this modern line-mass by Pat Morgart of Ormand Beach, Florida. Pink stargazer lilies join exotic hot pink ginger blossoms and palm fronds in a study of color and form and sweeping line.

right
Ann Payne of Mount Pleasant, South Carolina, has created a bold line design with points of massing. The vertical thrust begins at the base in a cluster of green anthuriums and foliage—Lenten rose, aspidistra, calathea, and holly fern—and is carried swiftly upward by sago palm, *Calathea lancifolia,* and sansevieria leaves (also known as snake plant or mother-in-law's tongue). A metal stand holds the top component.

above

Using only three kinds of plant material, Helen Goddard of South Dartmouth, Massachusetts, has executed a modern mass design in the style introduced by Italian designers. With characteristic blocking of one kind of plant material next to a contrasting one, Helen carries the eye from the bright and complex ginger blossoms to the smooth, looped aspidistra leaves that enclose space, to the layered monstera leaves. The opening in the container contributes to the feeling of mass and space.

opposite

The container, covered in handmade paper, is an integral part of this modern mass design by Ingrid Kelly of Houston, Texas. A ball of Oasis, covered in plastic and supported by a wire armature on the edge of the container, holds groupings of anthuriums, pincushion proteas, lotus pods, and beehive gingers. Scapes of arachnid orchids follow the line of the container, while dried New Zealand flax leaves enclose space and balance the asymmetrical placement of the mass.

overleaf, left

Rhododendron blossoms announce the color focus in this modern mass design by Kingslea Thomas of Houston, Texas. Calla lilies, the reverse side of calathea leaves, and liatris carry the message through the arrangement. The container, flax and ti leaves, and spikes of equisetum provide textural contrast as well as tints of lavender.

overleaf, right

Carole Bailey of Houston, Texas, used loops of green-twig dogwood to move the eye in and out and all around this massed arrangement in deepest to palest pinks—peonies, callas, stargazer lilies, and hydrangea blossoms. Spaces created by the loops alter the dynamics of the design, balancing the masses that rest—seemingly precariously—atop the tapering container.

9

in a different direction

The modern mass style offers a basis for contemporary designs that move in new directions—horizontally and diagonally.

page 204
The height of a wax container makes possible the sharp diagonal in this design of dark greens and burgundies. Susan Detjens of Sheffield, Massachusetts, centers her design with the tentaclelike form of an air plant (*Tillandsia* sp.), then establishes a strong diagonal line with layers of flax and calathea leaves, reinforced by alocasia, calla lilies, and arachnid orchids. The whole has a drama that is hard to imagine at any other angle.

opposite

Queen palm spathes shelter anthuriums in this horizontal design by Claudia Bates of Gainesville, Florida. Monstera leaves connect the two materials and add to the feeling of "Serenity," Claudia's name for the composition.

Reviewing the two hundred designs we have seen so far, it is interesting to note that the vast majority are arranged on the vertical. This is not so surprising in light of the American tradition of mass designs, even massed-line and line designs. A cylindrical container with a hole in the top certainly suggests inserting stems and extending the vertical direction. In traditional mass designs, a rule of thumb even recommends that the plant material should reach at least one and half times the height plus the width of the container. If we take a closer look at the preceding designs, however, we will see that a number of arrangers have taken a different direction, exploring how a less traditional placement can result in a very contemporary and creative look.

The modern mass design, featured in the last chapter, might be credited with encouraging American arrangers to embrace the horizontal as well the vertical. On pages 104 and 105 we saw how Margot Paddock and Jo Ann Wade used a square container, continuing the vertical direction of the sides. Using the same container, Helen Goddard (page 196), allowed the three masses of plant material to hug the horizontal top and extend beyond it. In a similar container (page 106), Susan Detjens used long leaves to create a strong horizontal thrust, then dropped a mass of blossoms down over the front of the angular container. (Extending Oasis above the rim of the container can facilitate this type of placement.)

In this chapter, two particular influences of the modern mass style will be evident—one a grouping of a single kind of plant material for impact, the other using only two or three kinds. (The latter is certainly a 180-degree turn from the Victorian and traditional mass designs, when more variety was to be desired in order to show the bounty of the garden.) Beyond these two recognizable characteristics, however, the sky—the horizontal sky—is the limit.

Let us begin by looking at containers that can comfortably accommodate vertical designs to see how arrangers changed the focus and the direction. The containers employed by Gail Emmons (pages 210 and 211) and by Renee Blaschke (page 214) illustrate how plant material, instead of being inserted, can be balanced across the top to dramatic effect.

By contrast, some—more contemporary, sculptural—containers practically demand a horizontal treatment. Certainly, the pottery pieces used by Margaret

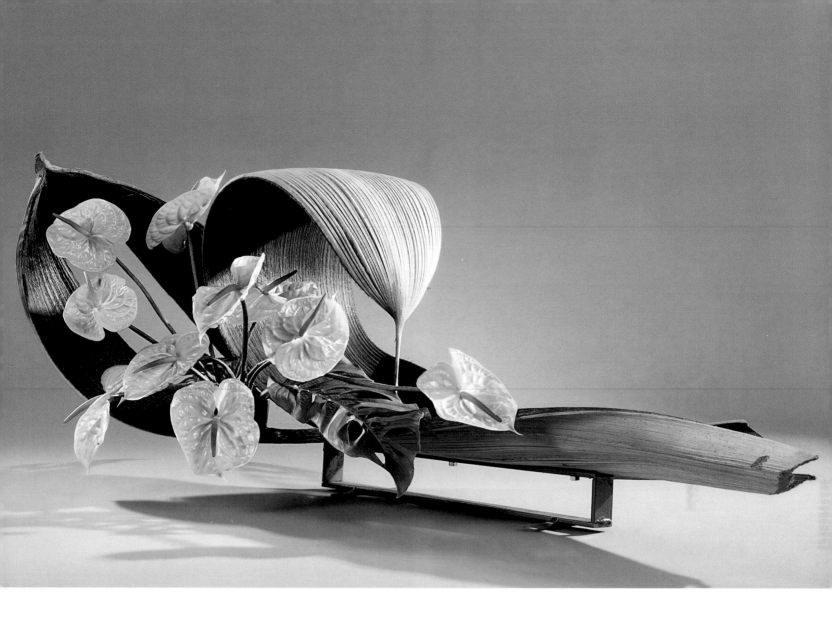

Ballard, Jo Ann Wade, and Trece Chancellor (pages 209, 215, and 216), seem at home with a horizontal placement, so much so that it is hard to imagine another direction.

A number of other horizontal designs in this chapter offer evidence that a container may be unnecessary. Claudia Bates's magical design of palm spathes and anthuriums (above), is elevated on a metal stand, but a container is neither needed nor desired. Similarly, Angela Raitano and Kitty Pottmeyer (pages 212 and 213), have positioned pieces of wood to their best advantage—on the horizontal—but without containers being part of the picture. (Cup holders that support the fresh plant material are not visible.)

Arrangers also take their designs in still other directions. Ann Payne explores the horizontal on two levels (page 208), then elevates a second design on a teepee of dowels (page 218), giving her the opportunity to follow the diagonal of the dowel lines with a thrust of clipped palms. Other designers—Lee LaPointe, Mary Ellen O'Brien, and Susan Detjens—show how arranging on the diagonal may be the only way to go.

above

This innovative and tension-filled design by Ann Payne of Mount Pleasant, South Carolina, is horizontal on two levels. Green anthuriums and dried sabal palm fronds all adhere to the horizontal plane but move out in opposite directions, leading Ann to suggest two possible titles for the design, either "Reaching Out" or "Bunk Beds."

above

Two containers act as one in this design by Margaret Ballard of Cornelia, Georgia. Two pieces of weathered wood provide horizontal direction, as do the calathea leaves, while sunflower blossoms add textural and color interest. Space, enclosed and implied, is a major component, begun in the overlapping containers and continued in the curves of the branches.

above

A metal Sogetsu Ikebana container allows Gail Emmons of Orinda, California, to layer mitsumata branches, creating a horizontal thrust. One branch on the vertical intersects the others and red anthuriums continue that line. A gently looped leaf of aspidistra contains the tension between the two directional forces.

above

When wisteria was blooming in her garden, Gail Emmons paired it with variegated flax leaves and a peeled and bleached manzanita branch placed horizontally across the top of a tall container. The wisteria blossoms drop naturally, the green of their racemes outlined against the neutral color of the container.

211

above

Bold, sculptural wood is shown to its best
advantage in this horizontal design by
Angela Raitano of Charleroi, Pennsylvania.
The wood, the rock outcropping, the
Pennsylvania skyline, and clusters of pink
rhododendron all led Angela to suggest
the title "Natural Jewels."

above

A twisted branch reaches across a
pool edged in stone in this horizontal
composition by Kitty Pottmeyer of
Pittsburgh, Pennsylvania. Chunks of glass,
clear and turquoise blue, move through
the design, accented by hosta leaves and
the bright blossoms of *Rhododendron
catawbiense* 'Roseum Elegans.' The glass,
according to Kitty, was found about thirty
years ago when she and a friend, both new
to flower arranging, would drive around
the countryside looking for interesting
material. They came upon a pile of glass,
discards from the nearby Pittsburgh Plate
Glass factory. She took these two, wishes
she had taken more, but, she says, they
were very heavy.

above

Renee Blaschke of Smithville, Texas,
has balanced a wisteria vine and two
heliconia blossoms atop a container by
potter Joanna Price in a bold horizontal
design. A single philodendron leaf unifies
the components and repeats the visual
importance of the spaces enclosed by the
twist of vine.

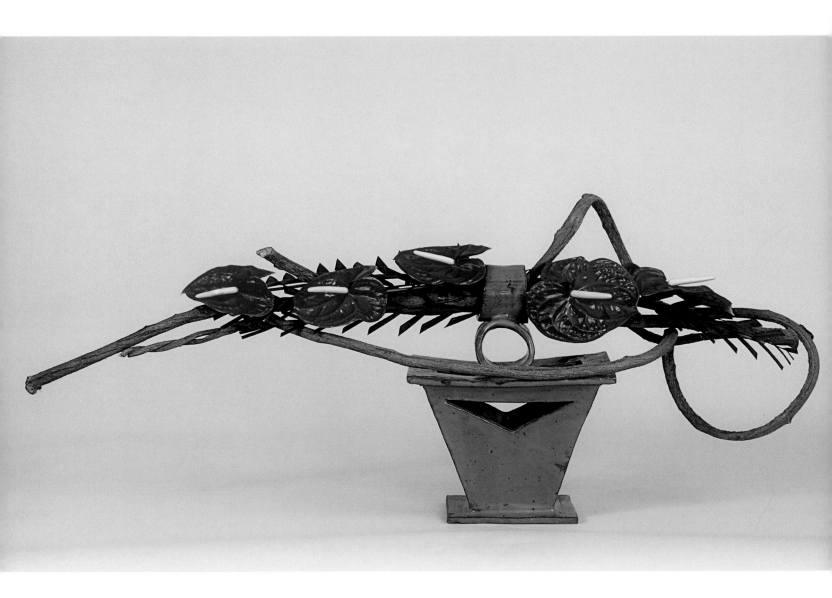

above

Trece Chancellor of Phenix City, Alabama, has created a tightly controlled horizontal design in which circles and triangles appear and reappear. One circle at the top of the container holds a wisteria vine, a clipped palm frond, and five anthuriums. Another circle and a triangular cutout are shapes repeated by the movement of the wisteria vine on its horizontal path.

above

A dried strelitzia leaf chose its own direction, but arranger Lee LaPointe of Vero Beach, Florida, paired it with an art glass container in a diagonal design that shows the best of both. White lilies repeat the curves without stealing the show, and a touch of baby's breath adds sparkle.

opposite

A sabal palm frond with its strong, pleated lines offers Ann Payne of Alpharetta, Georgia, the ideal material for exploring design on the diagonal. Dowels, held together by a rubber band, hold the palm and the flower form of a dried artichoke aloft while also sheltering more artichokes at the base. Lines, straight and slightly curved, dominate the design.

above

A roughly textured length of wood establishes the line in this diagonal design by Mary Ellen O'Brien of Sheffield, Massachusetts. Calathea leaves, the fiddleheads of ferns, and calla lilies follow the lead. Flax leaves go a step further and loop around to frame the central cluster of beehive ginger, alocasia, and fatsia leaves.

IO

exploring styles and techniques

*American arrangers seek out and embrace
design styles and techniques from
around the world—and invent
a few of their own.*

e have looked at designs with wood, cacti, and other natural materials and at designs with metals and plastics; at how a container can inspire, and how any one component can send creative imaginations in many directions. We have seen far-out and fine art complemented by floral designs, art-inspired exhibition tables, and "fine" jewelry made from seeds and beans. We have been reminded of the luxuriant beauty of period and traditional mass designs and seen the influence of the modern mass on horizontal and diagonal works. Now, in this final chapter, we examine additional styles and techniques that have gained favor with American flower arrangers.

PARALLEL PLANES

The parallel style, while hardly new, has a devoted following and myriad variations. Some versions—the vegetative, landscape, and gardenesque—are closely associated with Great Britain, but Judith Blacklock points out in *Flower Arranging Style* (1997) that Dutch florists arranged in the "Continental" manner—using the straight lines of market material—long before British designers adapted the parallel placement to garden material. The flexibility of the style becomes clear in the following designs.

CONTAINERS TIMES TWO

Six arrangers in this section explore the synergy that is possible when using two containers instead of one. Earlier examples of this were seen in Chapter 3, when Liz Shaw linked two containers with monkey ladder vine (page 76), and in Chapter 9, when Margaret Ballard overlapped open "squares" in a two-layered horizontal design (page 209). Designers in the parallel style frequently use two or more containers but in such a way that they blend as one.

MINIATURE MAGIC

Miniatures—designs measuring five inches or less—attract the same large crowds at the Philadelphia Flower Show as do the jewelry classes. And indeed there are similarities. Both require looking at the plant world in a new way—more closely than most have ever done before. Barbara Braman, writing in *GCA by Design*, conveys the enthusiasm: "Try miniatures if you want to rediscover the world around you and enhance your visual appreciation. It will change your life." Barbara and others emphasize that the same elements and principles of design that apply to any arrangement—particularly scale and rhythm—apply in spades to miniatures.

page 220

Reeds were soaked until pliable, then molded into a new sculptural form in this design by Pauline Flynn of Port Huron, Michigan. Openings hold balls of statice. The whole is supported on a large kenzan (needle-point flower holder) built by Pauline's son.

opposite

The striations on the surface of a resin container inspired Tasha Tobin of Akron, Ohio, to repeat and accentuate those lines with the contemporary technique of braiding. Bear grass was braided, then looped to form multiple layers and openings around a cluster of Voodoo roses. Tasha explains that she learned a refinement of the braiding technique at a Flower Arranging Study Group workshop in Paris with Marie Françoise Déprez. "Fencing" is the first step, with the ends of three strands of grass bound to the next three, then another three, and so on until you have a "fence." Tight, consistent braiding contributes further to the clean look and the undulating effect seen here. Time-consuming, yes, but the good news is, it dries beautifully.

TANTALIZING TECHNIQUES

During recent years, there seems to be a new technique introduced almost monthly, and American arrangers have been game to give each and every one a try. Words— *baling, banding, basing, bending, binding, blocking, braiding, bunching, bundling, clipping, clustering, collaring, facing, fencing, framing, grouping, hand-tying, lacing, layering, looping, mirroring, pavéing, petalling, pillowing, pleating, pruning, reflexing, rolling, sewing, shadowing, sheltering, shredding, spiraling, splitting, stacking, terracing, tiering, tufting, twisting, tying, veiling, weaving, wiring, wrapping*—and probably a few just coming into the vocabulary are as familiar as *conditioning* and *cutting* to many experienced arrangers. In the pages following miniature designs, you will see a number of these techniques executed, either singly or in combination.

NEW FORMS; NEW TIMES

Our final pages are devoted to arrangers who take existing plant material and create new forms. Pauline Flynn, Gloria Freitas Steidinger, and Claudia Bates (pages 220 and 248), work with plant material that has been soaked until it is pliable, then reshaped to the artist's will. Penny Horne has used a balloon—yes, a balloon—to help achieve the desired shape (page 249) . We conclude this look at the American way of flower arranging with additional examples of how arrangers in the United States seek out fashions from around the world, adopt and adapt them, and add innovations of their own.

above

Bold, exotic beehive gingers (*Zingiber spectabile*) tower over a carpet of roses, hydrangea blossoms, hypericum berries, and galax leaves in a parallel design by Tasha Tobin of Akron, Ohio. The papery pitcher plant (*Saracenia* sp.) and a wispy sedge catch the light in this gardenesque parallel in two containers.

opposite, above

In this spare version of the parallel, Ellen Wiley of Atlanta, Georgia, lets each variety of plant material have its own space—delphiniums, the bare stalks of carnations, flax leaves, the fiddlehead of a tree fern, the elongated blossom of an oakleaf hydrangea. On the lower level, three light-colored groupings—flowering cabbage, rhododendron, and hydrangea blossoms—are set off by dark expanses of galax, moss, and Lenten rose leaves.

opposite, below

Audrey Gonzalez of Memphis, Tennessee, introduced many American arrangers to the parallel style with this entry in the New York Flower Show in the late 1990s. Here, Audrey has used primarily traditional material for the vertical accents—chrysanthemums, asparagus ferns, ornamental pineapples, eucalyptus, calla lilies, hyacinths, liatris, alliums, carnations, and heather. But the tapestry at the base was another matter. The form, colors, and textures of the produce market took center stage—Brussels sprouts, red cabbages, radishes, mushrooms, squashes, and the ferny tops of carrots. Then, amongst the vegetables, Audrey tucked several amethyst geodes from Uruguay, where she is a member of the garden club and a champion for WAFA. The public was shocked by the unorthodox addition—and delighted. Some of us are still talking about "Audrey's mantel."

Parallel designs can take any number of directions. In this multilayered design by Helen Goddard of South Dartmouth, Massachusetts, elements go left, right, and straight up, creating an intricate but precise pattern. Costus stems lean right, pandanus leaves go left, and papyrus lifts its umbels above the cleanly cut ends of the other two. Smooth burgundy galax leaves, covering two of the trays, contrast with the color and texture of green trachelium in the third. In the background, leucodendron and wispy sedge increase the feeling of depth.

opposite

In a design that exhibits elements of both the parallel and synergistic styles, Susan Detjens of Sheffield, Massachusetts, has used five containers and a variety of plant material to create a green-and-white whole. Bells of Ireland, equisetum, flax, callas, fern, and dendrobium orchids establish the strong vertical emphasis while split and black-eyed peas provide support and interest at the base.

opposite, above

Why use one container when two could
be more interesting? Carol Swift of
Lake Forest, Illinois, chose two of the
same mottled glass in different shapes.
Anthuriums, ti leaves, and copper wire
appear in each, while a dried gourd
repeats the color of the glass and
presents a contrast in texture and form.

opposite, below

Two reed baskets designed to hang
on a wall are mounted on wooden
frames and treated as a unit by
Margaret Ballard of Cornelia, Georgia.
Peppers center the two segments, with
heliconias, anthuriums, and alocasia
leaves following the horizontal direction.
Green amaranth drops over the edges.

right

Carolyn Hawkins of Jonesboro,
Georgia, has bundled equisetum
with gold ribbon, inserting the longer
bundle in the shorter black container,
and the shorter bundle in the taller
one. Carnations reinforce the lines
with accents from the green-and-white
leaves of *Arum italicum*. Galax leaves
connect the two containers.

overleaf, left

Jeanne Nelson of Congers, New York,
uses two containers in a design titled
"Side by Side." A wisteria vine moves
from a small pot to encircle ginger,
flax, and anthurium leaves in a larger
one, enclosing additional space before
returning to its point of origin.

overleaf, right

Almost identical arrangements—of
hydrangea, anthurium, pittosporum,
succulents, hypericum berries, galax,
and dendrobium orchids—appear in
this two-part design by Ruth Crocker
of Cambridge, Massachusetts. Interest
is created by the difference in height of
the two glass cylinders, the equisetum
that lines the glass, and the swoop of
Flexi grass that moves from the top of
one to the base of the other, punctuated
by a green anthurium.

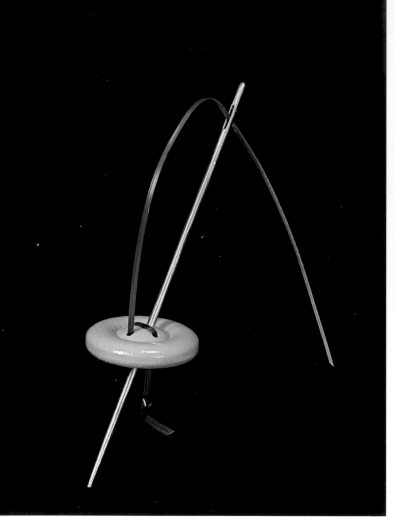

right

A miniature class at the Philadelphia Flower Show was titled "Trip to the Orient," and Leslie Purple of Wyndmoor, Pennsylvania, responded with an origami bird folded from a magnolia leaf. The bird and the black crescent moon, also covered in magnolia leaves, were painted gloss black and suspended in a niche lined with red matte board. Gold reeds made from *Clematis heracleifolia* vine and reminiscent of chopsticks point the way "to the Orient" and intensify the Asian feeling. As with so many miniature designs, the magic is in the suspension. Leslie explains: "The support system was stiff wire that I hot-glued to the back of the black disk, leaving about three inches projecting. I poked the wire through the back matte board, bent it over, and again hot-glued the bent section to the back of the board before inserting the whole into the mini niche at the flower show."

left

"Garment Industry" was the title of a miniature class at the Philadelphia Flower Show that set Gretchen Riley of Haverford, Pennsylvania, to "sewing." First she fashioned a button from a wooden disk and a five-inch needle from a dowel. All that was needed was one strand of bear grass—threaded through the needle, knotted on the end, and passed through the "buttonholes." What magical mechanic keeps it upright? The needle's point is stuck in foam board.

left
An acrylic container of multiple circles shimmers as green circles of spurge (*Euphorbia* sp.) weave in and out; the red of the stems is repeated in arachnid orchids and undulating wire. Marsha Webb of Atlanta, Georgia, achieved all this movement in a design just five inches tall.

right
A three-part container holds two sticks, three dried flowers, and a holly leaf. Repeating the circles that wrap around the container is a green Slinky-like wire. The Slinky resemblance is intentional. Sarah Stuver of Duncansville, Pennsylvania, lives just four miles from where Slinkys are made in Hollidaysburg, Pennsylvania. She created this miniaturized version by wrapping a wire around a pencil.

above

Loops of foxtail fern (*Asparagus densiflorus meyersii*) enclose space and frame pink roses above the rim of the container in this design by Claudia Chopp of Wentzville, Missouri. The roses that catch the eye, however, are the ones positioned along the length of an aloe leaf. Claudia has inserted the stems of the roses into the leaf, effectively turning the succulent into a source of water and nutrients.

opposite

Bobbi Heenan of Jefferson, Georgia, here creates an intriguing and sophisticated exploration of balance. The sharply defined open spaces on the left are countered by the filled but no less severe masses on the right. The smooth forms of small artichokes outline a rectangle that is only partially filled by green viburnum. This mass, in turn, is balanced by the large artichoke circled with viburnum at the top of the design, returning the eye to the negative spaces of the metal form, and back again to the large, dominant rectangle. Rhythm and balance; space open, closed, and implied.

above, left
Four frames showcase a collection of contemporary techniques in "Patterns" by Penny Decker of Ormond Beach, Florida. Equisetum is bundled; carnations—in a range of colors from pink to deepest burgundy—are pavéd; green and black alocasia leaves are layered. The yellow and green of pandanus appears repeatedly. The dark forms in the top and bottom frames are calathea leaves, turned to show their reverse side—another winsome way with plant material.

above, right
One metal frame merges into the next in this mélange of colors, textures, and techniques. Yellow lilies at the bottom give way to the brilliant scarlet of gladiolus. A circle of dahlias at the top incorporates the two colors and calls attention to the variegated pandanus leaves woven through the frame. A braided swirl of sabal palm points back to the lilies and the journey begins all over again in a design that Janice Hamlin of Bradenton, Florida, titles "Florida Sunrise."

opposite
Winsome could certainly describe this design by Liza Weihman of Steamboat Springs, Colorado. Two metal forms, one of which was seen earlier (page 53), provide the stimulus for taking off in new directions. Pink carnations, threaded onto pink Oasis wire, and Flexi grass (*Ficinia fascicularis*) loop from a lower hole in the left form, bypass all openings on the right, and return to the top left, there to join with a green spider mum and cymbidium orchid. Two catkins point to another green cymbidium suspended in space, courtesy of a water tube and a twist of wire. Liza says the cymbidiums represent a corsage and boutonniere in a design she titles "Prom Queen."

overleaf, left
Gretchen Riley of Haverford, Pennsylvania, has created a "French braid" from bear grass and used it to frame a single peony blossom. Hosta leaves, their parallel veining repeating the lines of the grass, form an underlying layer.

overleaf, right
Palm fronds lend themselves to braiding, too, as illustrated in this design by Bobbi Heenan of Jefferson, Georgia. The circles in the glass-and-ceramic sculpture are elongated and exaggerated in the curls of the palm and the fiddlehead of a tree fern. Leatherleaf fern backs the mosaiclike glass.

left

Three red-twig dogwood stems (*Cornus sericea*) are braced against a dark ceramic container from which a single pristine calla emerges. In this restrained, freestyle design by Joyce Overholzer of Fairfax Station, Virginia, more stems interweave with the original ones to create a screen that supports and showcases the calla.

right

Weaving describes the technique that Joyce Overholzer employed with just six finely variegated flax leaves. The resulting "fabric" shelters a partially opened amaryllis blossom emerging from one part of a complex handmade container.

opposite

Gloriosa or climbing lilies (*Gloriosa superba* 'Rothschildiana') meander through balls woven of bamboo strips held with thin plastic cable ties. Tension is created by the pronounced asymmetry of this Sogetsu free-style design balanced atop a tall container. Gail Emmons of Orinda, California, found the container, a piece of bamboo, washed up on the shores of a remote island in the Philippines.

above
Greens, pinks, and yellows move from the anthuriums on the left, to the carnations and chrysanthemum in the middle, to split aspidistra leaves on the right in this free-flowing design by Lynn Laufenberg of Waukesha, Wisconsin. Rosettes of galax leaves provide a point of pause, but the color and space in the aspidistra leaves continue to draw the eye.

Years ago, in the *Flower Arranging Study Group Newsletter* (now *GCA by Design*), Jane Morgan, a professor of Ikenobo Ikebana, described how to alter plant material in this manner: "Using your thumbnail, slit the aspidistra leaf along the vein toward the point, repeating several times, on both sides, working toward the outer edges. This will make the leaf flop and float like a cheerleader's pompom."

above

Bending is the technique used by Cecilia Lindemann of St. Charles, Missouri, in this design of space and lines titled "City Streets." Equisetum emerges from both parts of a ceramic container, moves up, down, across, and returns to one of the openings. Red gerberas offer color and contrast, but the angles and the enclosed spaces are the stars.

opposite

Ingrid Kelly of Houston, Texas, used the straight—and bendable—lines of equisetum to contrast with the curvaceous fiddleheads of ferns. The two crozierlike forms seem to be in a standoff on either side of a tightly massed group of equisetum. Tension reigns as other members bend over in defeat, or obeisance, or both.

opposite, left

Arranger Claudia Bates of Gainesville, Florida, fashioned these "irises" from the flower bracts of a split-leaf philodendron (*Philodendron selloum*). Spathes protect the spadix in these aroids, and Claudia collected and dried the outer coverings, then painted them the color of purple iris. It turns out Claudia and her fellow Florida arrangers have been making "hibiscus" from these spathes for some time. It was Claudia who wanted to try something new, and the irises are the result. After collecting the spathes, she soaked them, then coaxed the damp forms around two sizes of PVC pipe to get the desired curve. After drying, the "petals" were assembled into "flowers" and painted. In this arrangement, Claudia has paired the irises with purple bamboo and silvered curly willow, supported by a sculpture built by metal artisan Aubrey Griffis to her specifications. A single trimmed alocasia leaf repeats its curves.

opposite, right

Gloria Freitas Steidinger of North Easton, Massachusetts, has used the leaf bases from areca palms, called boots, to create new forms in a highly sculptural design. According to Gloria, the boots were curled by being soaked in the bathtub first, then rolled into the desired shape and secured with rubber bands. When dried, they were attached by hot glue to a rod secured to an iron base. Minimal amounts of contrasting material—date palm fruit and areca foliage—were then added to the design.

above

Light shines through skeletonized linden leaves in this new flower form by Penny Horne of East Rochester, New York, circled by looped aspidistra leaves. The magic is in the making. Penny begins with an inflated balloon painted with a mixture of glue and starch, then wrapped with string, much the way some hollow Easter egg forms begin. But the string is held to a minimum, and the delicate leaves are applied to the balloon's wet surface. Then, watchful waiting. "There is a moment," Penny reports, "between dried glue/starch and shrinking balloon when the balloon has to be popped. Otherwise, the fragile leaves will collapse inward as the balloon shrinks." Perfect timing results in a flower form to make Mother Nature proud.

acknowledgments

American floral designers embraced the idea of publishing a book on flower arranging that would showcase the creativity and diverse talents of our members. Over 1,000 photographs were submitted and 250 of the best have been selected for *Flower Arranging the American Way*.

We acknowledge and genuinely thank all the floral designers. Their artistic talents and abilities have enabled us to produce this book.

This is our salute to the members of the World Association of Flower Arrangers who have inspired us to become international designers. We thank all WAFA members for your enlightenment.

Nancy D'Oench, editor of this book, is known to many as a talented arranger, lecturer, demonstrator, and gifted writer. She wrote the text for *The Fine Art of Flower Arranging* and *Gardens Private and Personal*, which are publications of The Garden Club of America. We owe a debt of gratitude to this extraordinary lady for working countless hours from dawn to midnight on this book. Her efforts were given from a heart that overflows with kindness.

Mick Hales, a talented photographer, a gentle spirit and a man of fine character, provided the artistic skill to capture the beauty of the myriad of floral designs. His photography may be enjoyed in *The Fine Art of Flower Arranging; Gardens Private and Personal;* and *The Book of Psalms Illustrated*. Other gifted photographers contributed and are acknowledged in the photography credits on page 256.

We are especially grateful to the ten members of the WAFA USA Management Committee, who worked diligently to procure the funding for this book. A generous corporate contribution of $25,000 was made by SunTrust Bank. Other contributions were received by asking friends, family, and other floral designers to become subscribers for a $250 donation. Thus, this book is completely underwritten.

We are indeed grateful for every subscriber, because you have enabled us to use the income from the book to help us reach the financial goals enabling us to stage the 10th World Flower Show, "This Glorious Earth."

Thank you Day Companies staff—Jo Dollar, Joan Scott, Carole Smith, and Varion Spear—for providing logistical assistance.

We thank the leadership and the members of the flower arranging study groups. Your support has enabled us to move forward. The members of the Flower Arranging Study Group of The Garden Club of America and those of the Assembly of Flower Arrangers, composed of National Flower Arrangers and Creative Floral Arrangers of the Americas, affiliates of National Garden Clubs, Inc., have all worked together to make this book a reality. Thank you!

We extend our appreciation to Harry N. Abrams, Inc., publishers, and especially to Margaret L. Kaplan, Editor-at-Large, who mentored and encouraged Nancy D'Oench as the book progressed.

It was a privilege to be a part of this endeavor. My husband and I enjoyed hosting the seventy designers who attended the photo sessions. They traveled great distances to Atlanta, Georgia, in the southeastern United States to be present. Over a six-month period, ten to twelve designers per session came to our home, Bellmere, to work on floral designs. Each designer stayed two to three days and created numerous flower arrangements. It was a monumental task. Your dedication is greatly appreciated.

Other photo sessions were held in six states including photographing an entire flower show at the Dixon Gallery and Gardens in Memphis, Tennessee. We appreciate your commitment.

The WAFA USA Management Committee extends our sincere appreciation to every floral designer, the editor, the photographers, the book subscribers, the Day Companies staff, and all others who helped to make this book possible.

Flower Arranging the American Way is our gift and a way to say "thank you" to the member nations of WAFA that have encouraged us to enjoy flower arranging with friends from around the world.

Thank you for helping us celebrate "This Glorious Earth," the theme of the 10th World Flower Show.

Gratefully,

Deen Day Sanders

Deen Day Sanders
Vice President
Printing and Publications

Jackson, Dodie, Houston, TX

John, Sue P., Dallas, TX

Johnson, Carroll Taylor, Wilmington, NC

Johnson, Kathleen M., Dallas, TX

Jones, Jo Ann, Roswell, GA

Kelly, Ingrid, Houston, TX

Kelver, Bev, LaPorte, IN

Kindler, Pam, Rye, NY

Kummer, June M., St Louis, MO

Lake Forest Garden Club, Lake Forest, IL

Lamb, Bel, Beaumont, TX

Larkin, Kitty, Menomonee Falls, WI

Lea, Kathleen, Seattle, WA

Lewis, Betty, Hummelstown, PA

Lively, Loretta, Oak Hill, WV

Martin, Bonny, Memphis, TN

Martin, Helen S., Florence, SC

May, Barbara, Wayland, MA

McClendon, Babs, Alexandria, VA

McDaniel, Willie Mae, Decatur, GA

McDonald, Carol E., Monroe, LA

McMillan, Reverend William, DD, OBE, Belfast,
    Northern Ireland

McMurrey, Sue, Houston, TX

Middletown Garden Club, Middletown, CT

Mirmak, Bonnie, Vienna, VA

Monroe, III, Mrs. Walter D., Glenview, IL

Moor, Jr., Mr. & Mrs. Leslie M., Rockport, TX

Motzi, Crez, Downingtown, PA

Murken, Liz, Oshkosh, WI

Nalty, Elizabeth S., New Orleans, LA

Neely, Diana B., Medina, WA

Nicholson, Jessica, Lexington, KY

Nicolai, Shirley S., Fort Washington, MD

Noonan, Anne C., Greenwich, CT

Northbrook Garden Club, Northbrook, IL

Noyes, Ginny, Wilmette, IL

O'Brien, MaryEllen J., Sheffield, MA

Ogletree, Jimmy, Norcross, GA

Olson, Mimi, Kenilworth, IL

Osborne, Harriet H., Baton Rouge, LA

Overholtzer, Joyce E., Fairfax Station, VA

Paddock, Margot, Pittsfield, MA

Parrott, Sarah Belle, Roanoke, VA

Passfield, Nancy R., Port Sanilac, MI

Patterson, Sandra, Portola Valley, CA

Payne, Jackie, Alpharetta, GA

Pettit, Sally D., Worcester, MA

Piazza, Liz, Cold Spring Harbor, NY

Potter, Lula L., Beaumont, TX

Price, Maribeth, Milwaukee, WI

Pugh, Reggie & Patsy, Buford, GA

Purple, Leslie, Wyndmoor, PA

Raitano, Angela L., Charleroi, PA

Raymond, Mary Greer, Naples, FL

Reimers, Pamela, Greenwich, CT

Rhame, Lucy, Alexandria, VA

Rhode Island Judges Council of Rhode Island
    Federation of Garden Clubs, Inc., Tiverton, RI

Riley, Gretchen, Haverford, PA

Robertson, Joyce E., Murfreesboro, TN

Robinson, Sandra, London, KY

Roland, Cookie (Jacaline), Snellville, GA

Rosen, JoAnne, Seattle, WA

Runkle, Pauline, Manchester, MA

Sanders, Charles, Norcross, GA

Sanders, Deen Day, Norcross, GA

Schnack, Patricia, Honolulu, HI

Schreiber, Veva, Lake Bluff, IL

Schutz, Suzanne Cameron, Greenwich, CT

Scott, Joan, Atlanta, GA

Seale III, Julie & William, Dallas, TX

Seale, Katherine, Dallas, TX

Seale, Lucinda & William, Jasper, TX

Sedlacek, Pat, Cedar Rapids, IA

Shuster, Lois Dupre, Champion, PA

Smith, Carole, Duluth, GA

Spear, Dr. & Mrs. R. D., Dunwoody, GA

St. Peters, Don & Gerry, Indianapolis, IN

Stancill, Carolyn Ruth, Laurel, MS

Stephan, Molly B., Northfield, IL

Stephens, Emily Floyd, North Myrtle Beach, SC

Stephens, Kenn, Stratham, NH

Stewart, Katie, New Canaan, CT

Strawbridge, Mary Jo, Merion Station, PA

Stuart, Joy Walker, Atlanta, GA

Stuver, Sarah B., Duncansville, PA

Swift, Carol, Lake Forest, IL

Tate, Judy, Houston, TX

The 2007–2008 Garden Club of America Executive
    Committee, New York, NY

The Preservation Society of Newport County,
    Newport, RI

Thomas, Jr., Mrs. Sellers J., Houston, TX

Thomas, Kingslea, Houston, TX

Thompson, Virginia, Houston, TX

Tors, Linda S., Danby, VT

Trainer, Victoria, Lawrenceville, NJ

Trinkle, Dottie & Harold, Hardinsburg, IN

Truesdell, Charmane, Montpelier, MD

Turney, Donna, Alamogordo, NM

Van Allen, Marty, Green Village, NJ

Vanderzee, Jane Braqaw, New Canaan, CT

Vert, Char, Pasadena, CA

Vogel, Anna Lise, Livingston Manor, NY

Vollmer, Katrina, Nashville, IN

Wade, Jo Ann C., Phenix City, AL

Warshauer, Mary, Rumson, NJ

Webb, Frank & Bea, Norcross, GA

Webb, Marsha Pirkle, Sandy Springs, GA

Weihman, Mrs. Edward A., Steamboat Springs, CO

Westgard, Pat, Fargo, ND

Whetsell, Linda K., Tyler, TX

White, Woody & Jenny, Atlanta, GA

Whitmore, Marilyn L., Bedford, PA

Williams, Betty B., Norcross, GA

Williams, Bob & Gloria, Tucker, GA

Williams, Roger & Lola, Norcross, GA

Wilson, Rosine M., Beaumont, TX

Winnetka Garden Club, Glencoe, IL

Wood, June, Cedar Park, TX

Wrinkle, Louise A., Birmingham, AL

Youell, Glen, Bellevue, WA

Zaidan, Joy, Stone Mountain, GA

acknowledgments

American floral designers embraced the idea of publishing a book on flower arranging that would showcase the creativity and diverse talents of our members. Over 1,000 photographs were submitted and 250 of the best have been selected for *Flower Arranging the American Way*.

We acknowledge and genuinely thank all the floral designers. Their artistic talents and abilities have enabled us to produce this book.

This is our salute to the members of the World Association of Flower Arrangers who have inspired us to become international designers. We thank all WAFA members for your enlightenment.

Nancy D'Oench, editor of this book, is known to many as a talented arranger, lecturer, demonstrator, and gifted writer. She wrote the text for *The Fine Art of Flower Arranging* and *Gardens Private and Personal*, which are publications of The Garden Club of America. We owe a debt of gratitude to this extraordinary lady for working countless hours from dawn to midnight on this book. Her efforts were given from a heart that overflows with kindness.

Mick Hales, a talented photographer, a gentle spirit and a man of fine character, provided the artistic skill to capture the beauty of the myriad of floral designs. His photography may be enjoyed in *The Fine Art of Flower Arranging; Gardens Private and Personal;* and *The Book of Psalms Illustrated*. Other gifted photographers contributed and are acknowledged in the photography credits on page 256.

We are especially grateful to the ten members of the WAFA USA Management Committee, who worked diligently to procure the funding for this book. A generous corporate contribution of $25,000 was made by SunTrust Bank. Other contributions were received by asking friends, family, and other floral designers to become subscribers for a $250 donation. Thus, this book is completely underwritten.

We are indeed grateful for every subscriber, because you have enabled us to use the income from the book to help us reach the financial goals enabling us to stage the 10th World Flower Show, "This Glorious Earth."

Thank you Day Companies staff—Jo Dollar, Joan Scott, Carole Smith, and Varion Spear—for providing logistical assistance.

We thank the leadership and the members of the flower arranging study groups. Your support has enabled us to move forward. The members of the Flower Arranging Study Group of The Garden Club of America and those of the Assembly of Flower Arrangers, composed of National Flower Arrangers and Creative Floral Arrangers of the Americas, affiliates of National Garden Clubs, Inc., have all worked together to make this book a reality. Thank you!

We extend our appreciation to Harry N. Abrams, Inc., publishers, and especially to Margaret L. Kaplan, Editor-at-Large, who mentored and encouraged Nancy D'Oench as the book progressed.

It was a privilege to be a part of this endeavor. My husband and I enjoyed hosting the seventy designers who attended the photo sessions. They traveled great distances to Atlanta, Georgia, in the southeastern United States to be present. Over a six-month period, ten to twelve designers per session came to our home, Bellmere, to work on floral designs. Each designer stayed two to three days and created numerous flower arrangements. It was a monumental task. Your dedication is greatly appreciated.

Other photo sessions were held in six states including photographing an entire flower show at the Dixon Gallery and Gardens in Memphis, Tennessee. We appreciate your commitment.

The WAFA USA Management Committee extends our sincere appreciation to every floral designer, the editor, the photographers, the book subscribers, the Day Companies staff, and all others who helped to make this book possible.

Flower Arranging the American Way is our gift and a way to say "thank you" to the member nations of WAFA that have encouraged us to enjoy flower arranging with friends from around the world.

Thank you for helping us celebrate "This Glorious Earth," the theme of the 10th World Flower Show.

Gratefully,

Deen Day Sanders

Deen Day Sanders
Vice President
Printing and Publications

books by The Garden Club of America and National Garden Clubs, Inc.

RELATED BOOKS BY THE GARDEN CLUB OF AMERICA

D'Oench, Nancy, with coordination by Bonny Martin, and photography by Mick Hales. *The Fine Art of Flower Arranging: A Garden Club of America Book*. New York: Harry N. Abrams, Inc., 2002.

Flower Show and Judging Guide. New York: The Garden Club of America, 2009.

RELATED BOOKS BY NATIONAL GARDEN CLUBS, INC.

Kelver, Donn. *Gourds from Vine to Design*. Hong Kong: National Council of State Garden Clubs, Inc., 2000.

Harriet H. Osborne, editor. *Designing by Types*. Columbus, Georgia: National Garden Clubs, Inc., 2008.

Wood, June, and Marge Purnell. *The Essence of Floral Creativity*. Columbus, Georgia: National Council of State Garden Clubs, Inc., 1999.

Wood, June Pitts, and Deen Day Smith. *Table Settings for All Seasons, in the Home and in the Flower Show*. Columbus, Georgia: National Council of State Garden Clubs, Inc., 1995.

ALSO RECOMMENDED

Ascher, Amalie Adler. *The Complete Flower Arranger*. New York: Simon & Schuster, 1974.

Belcher, Betty. *Creative Flower Arranging: Floral Design for Home and Flower Show*. Portland, Oregon: Timber Press, 1993.

index

EDITOR: Margaret L. Kaplan
DESIGNER: Darilyn Lowe Carnes
PRODUCTION MANAGER: Anet Sirna-Bruder

Library of Congress Cataloging-in-Publication Data:
D'Oench, Nancy.
  Flower arranging the American way : a World Association of Flower Arrangers (WAFA USA) book / text by Nancy D'Oench ; coordination by Deen Day Sanders ; major photography by Mick Hales.
    p. cm.
  "Celebrating the 2011 world flower show This glorious earth."
  Includes index.
  ISBN 978-0-8109-4949-2 (hardcover)
  1. Flower arrangement, American. 2. Flower arrangement, American—Pictorial works. I. Sanders, Deen Day. II. Hales, Michael. III. World Association of Flower Arrangers. IV. Title.

  SB450.67.D64 2009
  745.92'240973—dc22

                        2008048900

Text copyright © 2009 Nancy D'Oench
Photo Credits
Unless noted here, all photos © copyright Mick Hales, 2009.
Jeannette Arrington, 84; Robin Baker, 61; Joanne Benning, 28; Tom Bettes, 214; Cheryl Collins, 161, 162, 164, 244; Digital Miles, 20 right, 39, 83, 228; Andy Foster, 30, 223, 240; Audrey Gonzalez, 225 bottom; Jim Jernigan, 4, 5, 12, 18, 20 left, 26, 27, 31, 33, 35, 44, 57, 59, 60, 63, 66 right, 70, 76, 86, 191, 194, 207, 237 right, 248 left and right; A. J. Kane and Robin J. Carson, 157; David Lavalley, 37 top; Whitney McNeill, 155; John Motzi, 8; Sandra Patterson, 156; George Post, 2, 72, 75, 210, 211, 243; Jan Pottmeyer, 213; Scott Rodgers, 15, 24, 25, 65 top and bottom, 66 left, 212; Tom Sherry, 6, 55, 91 left and right, 178, 223, 224

Published in 2009 by Abrams, an imprint of ABRAMS. All rights reserved. No portion of this book may be reproduced, stored in a retrieval system, or transmitted in any form or by any means, mechanical, electronic, photocopying, recording, or otherwise, without written permission from the publisher.

Printed and bound in China
10 9 8 7 6 5 4 3 2 1

Abrams books are available at special discounts when purchased in quantity for premiums and promotions as well as fundraising or educational use. Special editions can also be created to specification. For details, contact specialmarkets@abramsbooks.com or the address below.

THE ART OF BOOKS SINCE 1949
115 West 18th Street
New York, NY 10011
www.abramsbooks.com

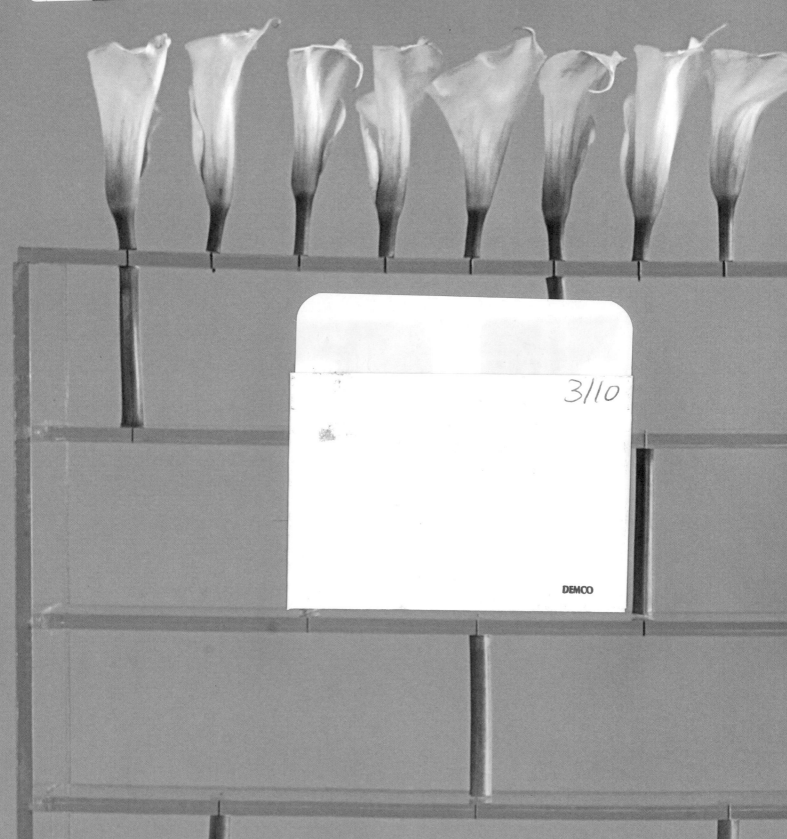